How to Win a Sports Scholarship

Penny Hastings
and
Todd Caven

REDWOOD CREEK
PUBLISHING

Santa Rosa, California

How To Win A Sports Scholarship
By Penny Hastings and Todd Caven

Redwood Creek Publishing
P.O. Box 368
Santa Rosa, CA 95402
www.winasportsscholarship.com

Although the authors and publisher have made every effort to ensure the accuracy and completeness of information contained in this book, we assume no responsibility for errors, inaccuracies, omissions or any inconsistency herein. Any slight to people, places or organizations is unintentional.

Printed in Canada

Library of Congress Catalog Card Number: 2006933754

Hastings, Penny and Todd Caven
How To Win A Sports Scholarship by Penny Hastings and Todd Caven—3rd ed., completely revised.

Summary: A complete handbook that takes high school student-athletes and their parents, coaches and counselors through the college sports recruiting process and teaches them how to maximize their chances of getting noticed by college coaches and offered a sports scholarship.
Includes bibliographical references and index.
ISBN-13: 978-0-9787132-2-5

College athletes—Scholarships, fellowships, etc.—United States—Handbooks, manuals, etc.

Acknowledgments

Teamwork is essential to winning a sports scholarship, just as it has been in our writing of this book. *How To Win A Sports Scholarship,* 3rd edition, was written using information gathered from over 1,000 college and high school coaches and athletic directors, current and former collegiate student-athletes and their parents, financial aid directors and high school counselors. Many of them are quoted in the book, and we are indebted to them for sharing their knowledge and experience with us.

To the hundreds of readers of the previous two editions who have contacted us with new information and stories of their success, we say: Thanks for telling us your stories and letting us know we helped you!

To our family and friends, especially Jennifer Caven and Mike Daniels, who encouraged and supported us: Without you, the game would have been over before it started.

Special thanks to Annette Gooch, for editing and giving pats on the back when we needed them.

Credits

Book design by Robert Marcus Graphics, Sebastopol, California; marcusgraphics@comcast.net
Printed by Friesens Book Division, Manitoba, Canada.
Printing consultant: Duncan McCallum, Spectrum Books, Santa Rosa, California.

Photo credits:
Bradley University
Oregon State University
Quincy University
University of Massachusetts
University of Nevada, Reno
University of Notre Dame
University of Southern California
Washington State University
Santa Rosa Junior College
Sonoma State University

About the Authors

Penny Hastings and Todd Caven have established themselves as experts in the field of collegiate athletic scholarships. Penny helped her son Todd develop a sports scholarship game plan that resulted in scholarship offers from several major universities, and Todd ultimately selected prestigious Stanford University, where he was awarded a soccer scholarship.

Following graduation Hastings and Caven carried out extensive research, including their College Recruiting Survey of over 650 college coaches, in addition to discussions with hundreds of high school coaches and counselors, college financial aid and admissions officers and student-athletes and their parents. Their personal experience and research convinced them that there was a strong need for a book to teach others how to wind their way successfully through the often confusing world of college recruiting.

They wrote the original book *How to Win a Sports Scholarship* in 1995. For the past decade they have received feedback from hundreds of student-athletes and parents, telling them that their advice saved their families hundreds of thousands of dollars in scholarship aid. This 3rd edition is the result of their experience and the input they've received from all over the country.

Penny Hastings, the mom, is a professional writer, instructor and consultant who lives in Northern California. She is the author of the book *Sports for Her: A Reference Guide for Teenage Girls,* Greenwood Press, 1999, and a specialist in women's sports and fitness. An advisory board member of the Women's Sports Foundation and member of the Bay Area Independent Publishers' Association, Hastings has written extensively for Knight Ridder newspapers, the *San Francisco Chronicle* and the *Press Democrat,* a Northern California paper owned by the *New York Times,* as well as other newspapers and magazines. She has been interviewed on radio and television and featured on an ESPN special on sports scholarships. She regularly presents sports scholarship seminars at high schools, club sports organizations and professional conferences.

Todd Caven, the son, graduated from Stanford University with a bachelor's degree in economics. He received his master's degree in business from Northwestern University and currently resides in Austin, Texas, with his wife and family of little soccer players. Caven works in commercial real estate investment and development.

To request information about consulting, presentations, seminars and group sales, go to www.winasportsscholarship.com or contact us at:

Redwood Creek Publishing
P.O. Box 368
Santa Rosa, CA 95402

Our Story:
How It Can Help You

We did it.
You can too!

Some high school athletes attract college scouts like bees to honey. They are bombarded with attention from college coaches in the form of letters, phone calls, e-mails, personal visits and ultimately, athletic scholarship offers. But what about the rest—the student-athletes who are not superstars but who want to continue to play their sport in college? Clearly, not all prospective student-athletes have "blue-chip" potential, so how do they attract the notice of college coaches and compete for scholarship offers? Is there a national database somewhere that college coaches access to find qualified student-athletes around the country?

These are some of the questions we asked when Todd first said he wanted to play his sport at the college level. At first we thought that if he were a good enough athlete, he would certainly be noticed by a college coach and offered a scholarship. But what if there was more to it than that? What if he wasn't noticed at all, but instead—overlooked? We decided that we could not afford to take that chance.

As we began researching the recruiting process, we quickly became frustrated by the lack of coherent information. We realized that there was no recruiting hotline, no central location where college coaches went to discover qualified student-athletes for their programs, no magical list. Many college programs, in fact, seemed to find their recruits haphazardly—through an associate of the athletic program or a chance encounter. This trend was even more apparent at smaller schools, many of which seemed to confine their search to a small geographical area due to limited recruiting budgets.

From our research and numerous discussions with coaches, guidance counselors, former and current collegiate athletes and their parents, we concluded that the student-athlete must initiate the recruiting process to avoid being overlooked. Armed with this knowledge, we began a systematic search for the right college, one where Todd could get the best education possible while playing his sport and receiving a sports scholarship.

We devised a game plan geared at marketing Todd and his talents to various colleges and their athletic programs. He contacted each coach and sent a packet of information about himself, which we subsequently called the Sports Resume Kit. He also indicated where the coach could see him compete. Soon he was swamped with replies from coaches, along with information about their schools.

While Todd was excitedly browsing college websites, pouring through college catalogs and talking with coaches, other talented student-athletes in our area were sitting back and waiting to get noticed. As a result, most were never contacted by a single college coach! These young men and women could have enhanced many a college sports program but they went completely unnoticed.

After receiving offers from four other colleges, Todd ultimately attended Stanford University on a soccer scholarship. While in college, he worked in the athletic department and helped to recruit student-athletes. From Todd's experience as an "insider," we learned why some student-athletes are vigorously recruited, while others—no less talented—are virtually ignored.

When we wrote the first edition of *How To Win A Sports Scholarship* in the mid-90s, it was because we wanted to share Todd's successful experience with other student-athletes. We revised the book in 1999, and this third edition of *How To Win A Sports Scholarship* is filled with the most up-to-date recruiting information available. We used the responses from our College Recruiting Survey, distributed to over 650 collegiate coaches across the nation—from the largest public universities to the smallest private colleges, and representing all 34 men's and women's sports in which scholarships are offered—to provide timeless tips and priceless advice on how to make your sports scholarship search successful.

Over the past 15 years we have talked to more than 1,000 high school coaches, student-athletes and their parents and guidance counselors. We have interviewed hundreds more former and current college athletes, athletic directors, admissions and financial aid counselors—all to gather the most current information.

Don't sit back and wait to be noticed!

Our greatest reward has been the scores of letters and e-mails we've received from readers over the years, thanking us for making available this step-by-step guide to college sports recruiting. While we cannot begin to know about all the student-athletes whom our book helped get into a college where they could play their sport and have scholarship assistance, we do know that many, many people who have bought *How To Win a Sports Scholarship* over the past dozen years have been glad they did!

Although recruiting has changed 180 degrees since we first became interested in the recruiting game, what remains unchanged is our message to student-athletes who want to compete at the college level: Market yourself! Bring yourself to the attention of college coaches! Don't sit back and wait to be noticed!

While we cannot guarantee that reading our book will earn you a sports scholarship, we can promise that by following the steps we have outlined, you will help create your own destiny rather than leave it to chance.

Todd playing soccer at Stanford University

Contents

1

Let Your Athletic Talent Take You to College

"Playing a college sport is a reward for all the hard work and dedication you, your parents and your coaches have put in throughout the years. At last, you have the opportunity to apply all that you've learned so far."

Russ Peterich
Coach, golf
Montgomery High School, Santa Rosa, California

A Solution to Rising College Costs

* Terms in bold italics are defined in the glossary

The skyrocketing cost of a college education is enough to send parents and students into a panic. With the price of *tuition**, room and board, books and supplies, transportation and other expenses escalating an estimated 6.5 percent a year, the average four-year degree could cost as much as $69,700 for a student entering in 2007-08. For private universities this amount could climb to $141,900, according to the College Board, a non-profit association of 4,500 schools, colleges and universities.

PROJECTED COST OF A COLLEGE EDUCATION*

Year	Public	Private
2006	16,357	33,301
2007	17,420	35,466
2008	18,553	37,771
2009	19,758	40,226
2010	21,043	42,841
2011	22,411	45,625
2012	23,867	48,591

* Adapted from the College Board's publication "Trends in College Pricing 2006."

Concerns over these spiraling costs can overwhelm parents and students. Some abandon the idea of college altogether, while others begin searching for outside sources of financial assistance. But, for *student-athletes*, a solution may very well be within their own reach.

Athletic Talent + Good Grades = Sports Scholarship

180,000+ scholarships awarded each year

Students with athletic ability and good grades can pay for all or part of their college educations with a sports scholarship. Scholarships are available in 34 sports played at the collegiate level—and not only in *revenue sports,* or *major sports,* such as football or basketball. From archery to badminton, crew to cross country, lacrosse to volleyball, athletic scholarships are available. The best news is that you don't have to be a *superstar* to win a sports scholarship!

If you are a better-than-average athlete and in the top third of your class, you could be eligible for any of over 180,000 athletic scholarships awarded each year by colleges and universities throughout the United States. Many of the scholarships offered are in non-revenue, or *minor,* sports, but there's nothing minor about the scholarship dollars they offer.

According to the *National Collegiate Athletic Association (NCAA),* the amount of scholarship money awarded each year for all sports in NCAA member *institutions* is over $1.2 billion. And that figure does not even include scholarships awarded by schools belonging to other athletic associations. For more information on athletic associations, see Chapter 3.

While scholarships are available to both men and women in most sports, some

$1.2 billion awarded yearly

sports and scholarships are available for men or women only. To find out if a sport is offered at a particular institution, consult one of the college sports guides on pages 164 and 165 in the Resources list. (More on researching colleges is found in Chapter 7.) Or go to the institution's website for information. A list of sports for which scholarships are awarded is shown in Table 1.

TABLE 1:
SCHOLARSHIP SPORTS

Archery	Football	Skiing, downhill
Badminton	Golf	Squash
Baseball	Gymnastics	Soccer
Basketball	Handball	Softball
Bowling	Ice Hockey	Swimming
Cheerleading	Indoor Track	Synchronized Swimming
Cross Country	Riflery	Tennis
Diving	Rodeo	Track & Field
Equestrian	Rowing (Crew)	Volleyball
Fencing	Rugby	Water Polo
Field Hockey	Skiing, cross country	Wrestling

These scholarship sports are only a portion of the competitive athletic programs at the collegiate level. Schools may also recruit athletes in such non-scholarship sports as martial arts, polo, power lifting, racquetball, water skiing, sailing and weight lifting.

At this point, your mind may be filled with questions:

- How do you know which scholarships are offered, and where?
- Do you qualify for one of those scholarships?
- How can you find out?
- Who can you talk to?
- Where do you look?
- When do you begin?

The answers to these and other questions about the process of winning an athletic scholarship are in this book.

Summary

⚽ As college costs are rising, parents and students are concerned about how they will pay.

⚽ Students with athletic ability and good grades can fund all or part of their college educations with a sports scholarship.

⚽ More than 180,000 college athletic scholarships are available each year in 34 sports.

⚽ To take advantage of the tremendous opportunities in intercollegiate athletics, student-athletes and their parents must be proactive.

You've learned that athletic scholarships can pay for all or part of a student-athlete's college expenses and are one solution to escalating college costs. Chapter 2 looks at and dispels four common myths that impede the search for a sports scholarship, throwing open the gym door to fantastic opportunities for talented student-athletes. ⏸➡

2

You Don't Have to Be a Superstar

"A student-athlete doesn't need to be a superstar. A lot of coaches are looking for the student-athlete with a strong work ethic, a team player who gives 100 percent and has a tremendous passion for the sport."

Sam Koch
Coach, men's soccer
University of Massachusetts

Dispelling the Myths

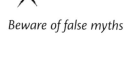

Beware of false myths

Student-athletes with potential often miss out on sports scholarships because they accept certain myths as "truths." They are often dissuaded from looking for a sports scholarship by the misconceptions of people around them, including players, parents, coaches, counselors and teachers. A mystique has evolved around the recruiting process, creating myths that far too many people believe. So, before we go any further, you need to understand why these myths are false. Here are the four most common myths:

Myth #1:   You have to be a superstar to win a sports scholarship.

Myth #2:   College coaches will automatically know about you if you are good enough.

Myth #3:   If you want a sports scholarship, you must have Division I talent.

Myth #4:   Female athletes have few scholarship opportunities.

Myth #1:   You have to be a superstar to win a sports scholarship.

Fact: Student-athletes other than superstars are awarded the majority of the more than 180,000 athletic scholarships that are available each year—more than twice as many if you consider that most scholarships are partial, divided up among athletes.

You don't have to be a superstar!

Only 1 percent of high school athletes get 99 percent of the attention from college coaches and recruiters. These superstars, commonly referred to as *blue-chip athletes*, have extraordinary athletic talent, along with high-profile scores, times and ratings. They top the list on scouting reports and are ranked state-wide and even nationally. However, there are just a handful of these superstars compared to the thousands of other athletes who make an important contribution to college sports teams each year. Even the most competitive colleges sign only one or two of these high-profile athletes in any given year, while less competitive institutions usually do not sign any of them but often still offer as many scholarships. So who gets these scholarships?

You do, providing you know how to go about it! College coaches fill their rosters with student-athletes whose past accomplishments prove that they are able to balance athletics and academics. They have shown the commitment, dedication and time management skills to excel in these different arenas. Read what these college coaches have to say to people like you.

Chris Bates, men's lacrosse coach at Drexel University, states, "One area college coaches are looking more seriously at is the student-athlete's dedication and commitment level. Participating in college athletics is not easy. It is very time-consuming and requires students to manage their time carefully."

"Contact several schools, including some schools with less competitive programs. Oftentimes a good player might help such a program while receiving a good scholarship," advises Ron Whitney, track and cross country coach, Santa Rosa Junior College, California.

"Show you can work hard academically, as well as athletically. Be a team player. I look for a strong work ethic, coachability and a positive attitude," says Sam Koch, men's soccer coach, University of Massachusetts.

Myth #2: College coaches will automatically hear about you if you are good enough.

Fact: College coaches will probably **NEVER** hear about you unless you bring yourself to their attention.

Thousands of young athletes across the country excel at sports in their hometowns and get their names in local newspapers. Although nearby college coaches may contact you as a result of local publicity, people outside your area won't hear about you unless **YOU** take the initiative and contact coaches at institutions you are interested in attending. Many high school student-athletes and their parents (and even their coaches) assume that college representatives will automatically read or hear about them. But consider the hundreds of thousands of articles in newspaper sports sections all over the country and you will realize that relying solely on local publicity is not a realistic way to get discovered.

Don't just sit on the bench

Some athletes seem to imagine that recruiters and coaches scour the countryside looking for talent. The fact is, even the most competitive schools and those with the biggest budgets cannot discover all or even most of the athletes who could make substantial additions to their programs. Many college athletic seasons overlap with high school seasons, so college coaches are often too busy with their own teams to search out new talent. Also, recruiting costs money. Many colleges simply do not have the budgets to search for athletes by traveling outside their local region.

The most important concept here for you to understand is this: If you sit back and wait, you will probably be overlooked. You have to get noticed to begin the recruiting process. To get noticed, you must market your talents.

While more than 180,000 college athletic scholarships are available each year in American colleges and universities, there may be five times that many college-bound athletes who qualify. With so many more qualified people than there are scholarships available, what determines who wins out? Is it pure luck? Not at all!

These scholarships go to *qualified student-athletes* who grab the attention of college coaches and maintain their interest through a concentrated marketing campaign, a well thought-out *game plan*. Just as you would put together a game plan for winning an athletic championship, you must put the same kind of thought and care into winning a sports scholarship.

Contact coaches yourself

Larry Rodgers, men's and women's cross-country and track coach, Pembroke State University, North Carolina, is impressed by athletes who contact him first. "Any athlete that promotes himself/herself shows a genuine interest in continuing his or her career and education," says Rodgers.

You have to find a way to let college coaches know that you exist and are interested in playing your sport at their school. You must make a concentrated effort to present yourself and your talents to coaches who will benefit from your addition to their team roster, but who, because of limited recruiting budgets and a lack of time, have never even heard or read your name.

Myth #3: If you want a sports scholarship, you must have Division I talent.

Fact: Over 180,000 sports scholarships are available each year, and not all are from Division I schools.

Many student-athletes consider only Division I schools, the highest level of collegiate athletic competition, when they think of sports scholarships. (More on athletic *divisions* is found in Chapter 3.) These schools are the ones you most often read or hear about and see on television. But, while these highly visible college sports teams draw the most attention, thousands of other colleges offer competitive sports programs and award athletic scholarships.

Don't limit yourself to Div. I schools

The story of David B., a 220-pound standout tackle on his west coast high school football team, is an example. David had his sights set on a Big Ten Conference school. A believer of myths #2 and #3, he waited to hear from one of these high-profile schools. Meanwhile, his senior year came and went. He had an outstanding season, yet not one recruiter from the high-profile colleges called or came to see him. Frustrated and bitterly disappointed, he finally enrolled in a local *community college*, where he excelled in the football program. He was recruited from that two-year institution and played his junior and senior years at a Division II school on scholarship. He could easily have played at the same school for his entire collegiate career, only the coach never heard about him while he was in high school.

Myth #4: Female athletes have few sports scholarship opportunities.

Fact: Scholarships and other intercollegiate sports opportunities for women continue to increase.

Legislation mandating equal sports opportunities for college women is partly responsible for the increase in scholarships for women. Furthermore, scholarships for women have been added in traditionally male-dominated sports, such as rugby and squash. Some coaches say they are having trouble giving away scholarship money available for these and a few other women's sports because currently there just are not enough women applicants. A major reason may be that many young women do not know these sports exist for them at the collegiate level. And since women's high school programs are only just adding these sports, there are not yet enough experienced participants.

Opportunities abound for female athletes

Pamela Bruemmer, equestrian coach, New Mexico State University, contends that the reason she has a hard time finding student-athletes experienced in her sport is that equestrian is so new to the collegiate athletic program, and most high schools don't offer an equestrian program. "We try to recruit girls who have been riding, but sometimes we take girls who don't have riding experience," she says. More about women's sports is found in Chapter 13.

Realizing that these myths are just that—myths—will put you ahead of the game and point you in the right direction to win a sports scholarship at the right college for you.

Summary

Four common but false myths have discouraged many students, parents, coaches and guidance counselors from looking into sports scholarships. The reality is:

- You don't have to be a superstar to win a sports scholarship or to compete in athletics at the college level.

- You have to make sure you get noticed by college coaches. You cannot just sit back and hope your phone will ring or a coach will arrive at your door with a scholarship offer in hand. It is up to you to market yourself—to let coaches at the colleges that interest you know that you have the ability and desire to play collegiate sports.

- High-profile Division I schools represent only a fraction of colleges throughout the nation where you can get a fine education and pay for it by playing your sport.

- Increased support for collegiate women's sports offers golden opportunities for women to compete for and win athletic scholarships.

Hopefully, at this point you are encouraged that an athletic scholarship is a possibility for you. But what exactly are athletic scholarships? Chapter 3 tells you just about everything you need to know. You will learn about the "hidden" benefits of sports scholarships, how scholarships vary and what you can do to maximize your chances for your scholarship to be renewed each year.

3

All About Athletic Scholarships

"From the beginning, I viewed college athletics as a way to help my parents pay for my education. My sport helped me get admitted to the colleges I was interested in and enabled us to pay the bills, too."

Chris P.
Former player, men's soccer
Stanford University, California

Benefits of Athletic Scholarships

For many student-athletes, being offered a sports scholarship is a boost to the ego, validation of their talents and a reward for many years of sacrifice and hard work. A sports scholarship is solid evidence that they are top-rated athletes. For others, it is a necessity when family finances cannot stretch to meet the costs of a college education.

Scholarships based on talent and potential

Athletic scholarships are based not on financial need but on athletic talent and potential. Offered by college athletic departments to prospective athletes as an incentive to play for that institution, sports scholarships are a primary recruiting tool in the highly competitive quest for the finest collegiate athletes available. Many student-athletes have received a college education they might not have otherwise experienced because their athletic talent resulted in a scholarship to pay all or a part of their fees and expenses. And, unlike other sources of financial assistance, athletic scholarships are not repaid. More on financial aid is found in Chapter 12.

Besides providing money and an affirmation of one's athletic excellence, athletic scholarships, the recruiting process and participation in collegiate athletics offer the student-athlete many advantages that nonathletes do not enjoy.

One advantage is preferential treatment in the admissions process. Recruited student-athletes often have an advantage over fellow students being considered for admission. They benefit by having someone pulling for them in the admissions process. A college coach who is interested in a particular student-athlete can recommend him or her to the admissions committee at the school. This is an extraordinary advantage. For the nonathlete, the written application must do all the talking, while the student-athlete has a personal advocate involved in the process.

Once admitted, the student-athlete may receive other benefits, such as student housing and preferred classes. Many schools set aside housing for student-athletes even when available space is at a premium. Entrance into preferred classes may also be a tremendous benefit, as practice schedules can narrow student-athletes' available time slots for attending classes. Too often nonathletes are forced to attend college longer than the standard four years because they cannot get the required classes when they need them, thus increasing their expenses.

Other benefits for scholarship athletes

In addition to assistance in admissions, housing and class selection, student-athletes are usually offered a wealth of support to help them both with academic and athletic concerns. Academic counselors and advisors specializing in athletics keep a watchful eye on the student-athletes assigned to them, ensuring they are making their grades and remaining eligible to participate in their sport while progressing satisfactorily towards graduation. Student-athletes are encouraged to use other important student services, such as tutoring programs and mentors. Some colleges have computer labs set up within the athletic complex for the exclusive use of student-athletes. Additional services coordinated between other college departments and the athletic department give student-athletes the best possible chance for academic and athletic success.

There are also other benefits, suggests Stan Morrison, athletic director, University of California, Irvine: "Something never to be taken for granted is the 'built-in family' a college team provides to student-athletes from the first day they arrive on campus, an instant support network to help often homesick kids 'learn the ropes'."

Morrison adds: "Coaches and athletic administrators are great for opening doors for student-athletes to meaningful employment after graduation and summer employment."

A Brief History of College Athletics and the Sports Scholarship

College recruitment of student-athletes began in the 1880s as college football began its transition from an extracurricular recreational activity to a highly commercialized sport. Prior to the turn of the century, compensation for collegiate athletes usually took the form of employment, free lodging, meals, gifts and other special favors. Primarily funded by a school's alumni and fraternities, player compensation was offered to provide the incentive to compete for a particular school and to perform at the highest level possible. The promise of payment was most often a verbal pledge to the athlete that he would be well cared for.

As college football quickly became popular, many institutions around the country built gigantic structures to house the fast-growing sport. Harvard's was the first stadium, built in 1903. Winning became increasingly important. Along with garnering prestige for a college, a winning team generated greater attendance at games and more money.

The emphasis on winning sports programs created a heavy demand for each year's available athletic talent, not only for football, but in other sports growing in popularity, including track, rowing and baseball. With so many colleges looking to expand their appeal to potential students and donors, competition for gifted athletes increased, resulting in greater financial rewards being offered to student-athletes in an effort to attract them. The modern age of collegiate athletic recruiting had begun.

Throughout the first half of the 20th century there were numerous calls for a return to purely *amateur* sports because of unfair recruiting practices brought about by the fierce competition among colleges. In 1952, the National Collegiate Athletic Association (NCAA) legalized the use of athletic scholarships for the purpose of attracting qualified student-athletes and at the same time established national college athletic standards, including the limit on the amount of compensation a student-athlete could receive.

"Recruiting has become more sophisticated with each passing year," relates John F. Rooney, Jr. in his book, *The Recruiting Game*. "Ever-increasing pressures to win, combined with limitations on the number of scholarships that can be awarded have made the recruiting process both more important and more difficult than ever." More on recruiting rules is found in Chapter 11.

Intercollegiate Athletic Associations

Intercollegiate *athletic associations* are organizations made up of colleges and universities that administer all areas of intercollegiate athletics, including recruitment policies, the *eligibility* of student-athletes and *financial aid.* Most colleges belong to either the National Collegiate Athletic Association (NCAA), *National Association of Intercollegiate Athletics (NAIA)* or the *National Junior College Athletic Association*

(NJCAA). There are also other, smaller associations. Because each association has different rules and policies, you should ask the coaches at colleges that interest you about their athletic association affiliation.

NCAA

The NCAA is the largest and best known of the associations. Formed in 1906 in response to the need for reform after severe injuries and deaths occurred on the nation's college football fields, today the NCAA has a membership of over 1,000 four-year institutions, ranging from the largest state universities to small private colleges.

There are three divisions in the NCAA: Divisions I, II and III. The major differences among NCAA divisions include academic and eligibility standards and financial aid limitations, as shown in Table 2.

TABLE 2:
NCAA DIVISIONS

Division I	Division II	Division III
Typically very competitive	Sometimes less competitive	Often less competitive
Mostly major colleges and universities	Generally smaller colleges and universities than Division I	Generally smaller colleges and universities than Division I
Athletic scholarships awarded	Athletic scholarships awarded	No athletic scholarships awarded (all financial aid based on need)

NAIA

The NAIA is the second largest intercollegiate athletic association, with nearly 300 four-year member colleges in the U.S. and Canada. The NAIA, which held its first championship event more than a half-century ago, has two divisions, I and II.

NJCAA

Each institution belonging to the NJCAA, an association of 500 member two-year colleges, competes in one of three divisions—I, II or III— in designated sports. Many Division I and II programs award athletic scholarships, while Division III is prohibited from offering sports-related financial assistance.

Athletic Conferences

Athletic conferences, such as the Pac-10 or Big East, are collections of collegiate institutions joined together for the purpose of enhancing athletic competition among member schools. These conferences usually belong to an athletic association and may have their own rules regarding recruiting, competition and scholarships. To find out in which athletic conferences specific schools compete, call the schools directly or visit their websites.

Types of Scholarships Available

Full vs. Partial Scholarships

Athletic scholarships range from "top-of-the-line" full scholarships (popularly referred to as a *full ride*) to partial scholarships. Full athletic scholarships cover actual educational costs, including tuition and fees, room and board and required books and supplies, while partial scholarships might cover only a portion of these costs.

Many scholarships divided between athletes

Partial scholarships are full scholarships that are divided among several players. Although partial scholarships allocate less money to each student-athlete, they allow athletic programs to provide financial assistance to more players. Division I University of Massachusetts allots the equivalent of two men's full soccer scholarships each year. Says head soccer coach Sam Koch, "We divide up the scholarships. We feel it is better to award a portion to a few players rather than a full scholarship to only two. It gives us a better chance to compete for recruits and help more players."

Number of Scholarships Available

Athletic associations set the maximum number of scholarships that can be awarded in a sport in different divisions. For instance, the NCAA allows a member school a maximum of 9.9 scholarships to be awarded each year for men's Division I soccer. However, each college program sets its own athletic budget and decides how many scholarships it can afford to offer in a sport up to the association maximum. A particular Division I men's soccer program may choose to offer less than 9.9 scholarships or none at all.

Athletic conferences also set a limit on the number of scholarships that can be awarded in a sport for member institutions. In some cases, the limit may be lower than that set by the athletic association to which the conference belongs.

Number of Scholarships Offered Can Change

The number of scholarships offered may vary year to year at an institution, depending upon a variety of factors, such as the athletic department budget and the financial needs of the institution's other athletic programs. After determining whether the schools you are interested in offer scholarships in your sport, ask the coaches how many scholarships are usually given each year and whether they see that number changing in the future. Remember that although athletic associations such as the NCAA mandate the maximum number of scholarships that may be given in a sport, the member institution decides how many to offer, if any. It is important to understand that the number of scholarships may change from year to year at any given school due to reasons beyond your control.

Schools determine number of scholarships awarded

A list of NCAA sports and the maximum number of scholarships allowed in each is found in Table 3, page 16. The maximum number of scholarships is not applicable in NCAA Division III sports, as athletic scholarships are not awarded. In Chapter 7, you will find out how to determine which schools offer scholarships in your sport.

TABLE 3:
NCAA SPORTS AND SCHOLARSHIPS

Division I Men's Sports

Baseball	11.7	Rifle	3.6
Basketball	13.0	Skiing	6.3
Cross Country/Track	12.6	Soccer	9.9
Fencing	4.5	Swimming	9.9
Football	85.0	Tennis	4.5
Golf	4.5	Volleyball	4.5
Gymnastics	6.3	Water Polo	4.5
Ice Hockey	18.0	Wrestling	9.9
Lacrosse	12.6		

Division I Women's Sports

Archery	5.0	Rowing	20.0
Badminton	6.0	Rugby	12.0
Basketball	15.0	Skiing	7.0
Bowling	5.0	Soccer	14.0
Cross Country/Track	18.0	Softball	12.0
Equestrian	15.0	Squash	12.0
Fencing	5.0	Swimming and Diving	14.0
Field Hockey	12.0	Synchronized Swimming	5.0
Golf	6.0	Team Handball	10.0
Gymnastics	12.0	Tennis	8.0
Ice Hockey	18.0	Volleyball	12.0
Lacrosse	12.0	Water Polo	8.0

Division II Men's Sports

Baseball	9.0	Rifle	3.6
Basketball	10.0	Skiing	6.3
Cross Country/Track	12.6	Soccer	9.0
Fencing	4.5	Swimming and Diving	8.1
Football	36.0	Tennis	4.5
Golf	3.6	Volleyball	4.5
Gymnastics	5.4	Water Polo	4.5
Ice Hockey	13.5	Wrestling	9.0
Lacrosse	10.8		

Division II Women's Sports

Archery	9.0	Rowing	20.0
Badminton	10.0	Rugby	12.0
Basketball	10.0	Skiing	6.3
Bowling	5.0	Soccer	9.9
Cross Country/Track	12.6	Softball	7.2
Equestrian	15.0	Squash	9.0
Fencing	4.5	Swimming and Diving	14.0
Field Hockey	6.3	Synchronized Swimming	5.0
Golf	5.4	Team Handball	12.0
Gymnastics	6.0	Tennis	6.0
Ice Hockey	18.0	Volleyball	8.0
Lacrosse	9.9	Water Polo	8.0

Athletic Scholarship Renewal

Sports scholarships are renewed yearly

Athletic scholarships currently are limited one-year awards and are renewable on an annual basis. The four- or five-year "free ride" is a thing of the past. According to the NCAA, athletic scholarships are awarded for one academic year only. Each year the athletic department may renew the scholarship for an athlete up to a maximum of five years within a six-year period, but renewal is not automatic.

NCAA and other association rules allow *recruits* to be told that the athletic department will recommend renewal of the aid each year and that such recommendations have generally been followed in the past. But renewal is not fully guaranteed, and a prospective student-athlete must understand that certain circumstances may warrant its nonrenewal. Although criteria for renewal of athletic scholarships are strictly regulated by the NCAA and other associations to protect the interests of both the student-athlete and the college, you should talk with coaches and the financial aid offices of the schools that interest you about criteria for scholarship renewal.

An appeal process is mandated by NCAA for any student-athlete who believes that the reduction or withdrawal of scholarship aid is not merited. An impartial committee reviews the details of the appeal and makes a decision. See NCAA website for more details.

Athletic Scholarships Are Only One Form of Financial Aid

Check out financial aid

Athletic scholarships are often combined, or packaged, with other sources of financial aid. (More on financial aid is found in Chapter 12.) *Financial aid packages* are designed to combine aid based on financial need with other awards. Combinations may include a sports scholarship, state and/or federal government grant, an academic scholarship from the college or a scholarship from a private club or organization, along with an *educational loan* and a *work-study* award. University of Iowa's financial aid director Mark Warner explains: "Our office works closely with the men's and women's athletic departments. When a coach lets us know about a student to whom an athletic scholarship is being offered, we check out the student's financial status. If the scholarship covers all the student's financial need, then nothing else is awarded. If it doesn't, then a financial aid package is put together to cover that need."

Summary

🔘 Many athletes have received a college education they might not otherwise have been able to afford as a result of a full or partial sports scholarship.

🔘 Special benefits for recruited student-athletes may include having a personal advocate in the admissions office, guaranteed housing and preferred class registration.

🔘 Intercollegiate athletic associations such as the NCAA administer intercollegiate activities, including recruiting, eligibility requirements and financial aid.

🔘 Full athletic scholarships are generally offered to the most gifted of student-athletes; the majority of awards are for partial scholarships.

🔘 Athletic scholarships are not repaid and can often be supplemented with other forms of financial aid for students who qualify.

You have learned what athletic scholarships are and in which sports they are available. But, how do you know if you have what it takes to win a sports scholarship? Chapter 4 tells you how to assess your athletic potential so you can more accurately consider your chances.

4

Do You Have What It Takes?

"Understand through talking with your coaches and parents at what level you can be both comfortable and challenged—in your sport and in the classroom."

David Harris
Coach, men's/women's track and cross-country
Emporia State University, Kansas

How Do You Know If You're Good Enough?

Before embarking upon the quest for athletic scholarship dollars, you need to determine your potential for participating in collegiate athletics. How do you know if you are talented enough for college sports? At which level of competition could you expect to play? Where would you feel most comfortable?

Following these three steps will help you gain a realistic picture of your chances:
- Take a good, hard look at yourself.
- Compile and compare your *statistics*.
- Seek the advice of others.

Take a Good, Hard Look at Yourself

Are you good enough?

Understanding yourself as an athlete is important. You need to look at where you stand in comparison to others and learn about the demands typically associated with collegiate athletics.

The following questions have been compiled with the help of both current and former collegiate coaches and athletes to help you assess your athletic potential and provide insight into some of the qualities and traits important for success in the world of college sports.

So sit down with a sharp pencil, read the questions on page 20 and answer them as realistically as possible. If you are a multi-sport athlete, answer these questions for each sport. Answering some questions will require the assistance of others, as discussed later in this chapter.

ATHLETIC SELF-ASSESSMENT QUIZ

❑ Yes ❑ No   1. Am I recognized as an above-average athlete in my sport at the high school level? Club level? Regional level? National level?

❑ Yes ❑ No   2. When I compete against other college-bound athletes in my sport, do I feel I am at the same skill level? If not, do I see myself as having the potential for achieving that level?

❑ Yes ❑ No   3. If I have had a chance to compete against current college athletes in my sport, do I feel I am at the same skill level? If not, do I see myself as having the capability to achieve that level?

❑ Yes ❑ No   4. Do I work hard to correct those areas in which I feel I am below average?

❑ Yes ❑ No   5. Am I a competitive person?

❑ Yes ❑ No   6. Am I able to function better than most others in a competitive environment?

❑ Yes ❑ No   7. Does my body respond positively to physical exertion without suffering repeated injuries?

❑ Yes ❑ No   8. Am I able to function at a high athletic level on a day-to-day basis?

❑ Yes ❑ No   9. Do I set goals and strive to meet them even if it takes longer than I originally expected?

❑ Yes ❑ No   10. Am I able to manage my time effectively so that I usually can meet nonathletic demands in a timely manner?

❑ Yes ❑ No   11. Am I willing to forgo social or other extracurricular activities, if necessary, in order to meet athletic and academic deadlines and requirements?

❑ Yes ❑ No   12. Do I consider myself to be "coachable"?

❑ Yes ❑ No   13. If my sport is an individual sport, am I able to spend long hours, possibly alone, practicing?

❑ Yes ❑ No   14. If my sport is a team sport, am I able to spend long hours with the same people during practice, travel and other events?

❑ Yes ❑ No   15. Most of the time, do I look forward to practicing my sport?

❑ Yes ❑ No   16. Have I received recognition in my sport in the form of awards, honors and newspaper articles or other media coverage?

❑ Yes ❑ No   17. Have my own coaches or opposing coaches acknowledged my athletic ability and suggested that I may have the ability to compete at the collegiate level?

❑ Yes ❑ No   18. Am I able to focus upon the task at hand even though I may be involved in numerous other activities or projects at the same time?

❑ Yes ❑ No   19. Can I accept the possibility that I may not be the best athlete on my team in college and that I may have to wait my turn before getting a chance to play?

❑ Yes ❑ No   20. Do I understand that I will be enrolled in college for an education and that athletics, while important, is not the only reason I will be attending?

If you can answer yes to most of the above questions, you may have what it takes to compete at the collegiate level.

Compile and Compare Your Statistics

A good way to assess your athletic abilities is to compare them to those of other athletes in your sport. One method of doing this is to look at your athletic statistics. Statistics differ from sport to sport. If you do not know what stats are important in your sport, ask your high school or *club team* coach. They have probably been recording your stats all along or can help you begin to compile them.

Another possible source of statistical information is your parents, who may have boxes of keepsakes or scrap books for articles and honors collected during your athletic career. If these are not available, back issues of your school or town newspaper, or a web search can also be excellent sources of statistics you can use. Beginning to compile your stats early, in addition to helping you assess your potential, will help you later on in the recruiting process, as college coaches will undoubtedly want to know this information.

Once you have compiled your stats, you can use them to compare yourself to other athletes. For instance, you might compare goals scored, yards rushed, event times, batting averages, etc. Having this information will give you a good indication of where you stand in relation to others.

Pete Hovland, men's swimming coach, Oakland University, Missouri, has some advice on the self-assessment process: "Be realistic. If you're not competitive as a senior in high school...don't expect a scholarship."

Seek the Advice of Others

Ask the experts

In order to gain additional insight into your chances for participation in collegiate athletics, it is important to enlist the help of others who are familiar with you and your athletic abilities. People who can help you include:

- your high school and/or club team coaches
- coaches from opposing teams
- college coaches
- other coaches who have seen you compete
- current or former college athletes

Your high school and/or club team coaches

High school and club or elite team coaches who have worked with you probably know your skills better than anyone else. Getting an honest assessment of your talents from them can be invaluable. They can go over your statistics with you, let you know how they feel you compare not only with other college-bound athletes, but with current and former college athletes they have coached, and give you their opinion about your potential to compete at the collegiate level. They can also indicate what they think are your weaknesses, as well as your strengths. With this information you can work to make necessary improvements.

Compare your stats to others

You may feel uncomfortable about approaching your coach and asking, "How good am I?" It takes courage to risk the possibility that a coach might tell you he or she doesn't think you're college-level sports material. However difficult this may be, your coaches' opinions and involvement are of vital importance throughout the recruiting process, as will be discussed in later chapters.

Coaches from opposing teams

Coaches from opposing high schools and clubs can often provide you with information about how you are perceived in the local sports community. They can furnish an assessment of your skills from a different, sometimes more objective, perspective than your own coach. Russ Peterich, golf coach and former athletic director at Montgomery High School in Santa Rosa, California, states that while he is not often asked by athletes from other schools for his assessment of their collegiate athletic possibilities, he is very willing to talk to them or their parents: "I can give an objective viewpoint. I see them perform, have to figure out how to best compete against them and observe how they measure up against my own players. Talking to opposing coaches is very helpful for the student-athlete looking towards competing at the college level."

Coach Peterich encourages parents to talk with him about their sons' or daughters' athletic abilities: "Sometimes parents have unrealistic expectations, and that puts a lot of pressure on their kids. It's hard enough for kids to decide if they have what it takes to play college sports. I try to be encouraging, but also realistic. It helps if the parents and the athlete are on the same wavelength."

College coaches

Be realistic

If you are fortunate enough to know any college coaches who are familiar with your athletic ability, they can help you from yet another perspective. Being involved with college athletics on a daily basis, they are aware of what it takes to succeed and can suggest the level of competition at which you would be most comfortable. Also, college coaches talk with each other and with high school coaches about up-and-coming athletes. Most coaches are glad to be asked their opinions and will be honest with you about your chances.

"I'm happy to talk to student-athletes about their college sports potential. If a kid plays anywhere within 100 miles or so, I've probably watched her and talked to her coach. If I have not seen her play already and she asks for an assessment, I would make an effort to see her at a local event or tournament." says Shellie Onstead, women's field hockey coach, University of California at Berkeley.

Other coaches who have seen you compete

Other coaches, including sports camp coaches, summer team coaches and all-star or select team coaches, might also be helpful. Make an effort to contact them and ask about your chances of competing at the collegiate level. Even if your contact with them is not recent, they may be familiar with your athletic progress.

Current or former college athletes

If you know any student-athletes who are already competing in your sport at the college level or who have had college sports experience, call or e-mail them and ask about their experiences. Even if you don't know someone personally, ask around and find the names of local athletes who have blazed the trail before you. Call them and let them know you are thinking about participating in college sports and trying to assess your possibilities. Listen and ask questions. Understanding how they were perceived in your local sports area and how they are faring in the larger, more competitive collegiate arena can help you to gauge your own skills and college potential.

Draw Conclusions Based on Your Athletic Assessment

At this point, if you've thought about and answered the questions in our Athletic Self-Assessment Quiz, compared your statistics with those of others and sought the advice and opinions of former and current coaches and college athletes, you probably have a pretty good idea of your collegiate sports potential. If the outlook is positive, you are ready to move on to the next step: assessing your academic potential.

If the picture doesn't look quite as rosy at this point as you would like, there's still hope. Don't give up! You know now what you have to work on to improve your skills, fitness or overall understanding of your sport. If you are young, you have plenty of time to make these improvements. If you are closer to college age and your chances of qualifying for a scholarship don't look too promising, you still have options that could enable you to participate in your sport.

You can go to a non-scholarship school or compete at a less competitive level. Or you can consider a two-year community college, where you can continue to improve with the possibility of being recruited and later transferring to a four-year school that offers scholarships in your sport. More on community colleges is found in Chapter 7.

Regardless, you are now better informed about your athletic skills and the possibility of qualifying for a sports scholarship. But one thing you may not know is what college sports are really like. Up to this point, you may have been concentrating all your efforts on assessing your potential, but do you really have a clear idea of what playing a sport in college involves? The following section will give you some insight from those who have been there.

The Demands of College Sports: Student-Athletes Speak

In many interviews college athletes have agreed that one of the biggest challenges they faced when they got to college was time management. Mark S., former Stanford University *varsity* soccer player emphasizes this point: "Probably the most difficult adjustment you make as a student-athlete is to learn to balance all your competing needs—academic, athletic and social—particularly in your first semester at school. The step one takes from high school to college is a giant one."

Besides being on their own for what may be the first time in their lives, first-year college students have to adjust to being away from home in an unfamiliar environment, learning new ways of doing things and meeting people from all over the world, as well as being forced to rise to higher academic challenges. In addition to having to make the jump to college academics, the student-athlete has to make the leap from high school to college-level sports.

"Perhaps the biggest surprise of my college career was the tremendous amount of time and effort it takes to be a full-time player within a competitive program at the Division I level," Mark discloses. "During the actual playing season, there is relatively little free time. Beyond participating in your sport—practice and game time, weight room sessions, travel time, community appearances, team meetings—there is your class and study time."

While college sports have their primary season, such as football in the fall, basketball and volleyball in the winter and track and baseball in the spring, most coaches hold practices in *off-season* periods and generally expect the student-athlete to participate during the entire school year.

Mark S. reflects, "It is a popular perception that the off-season affords you some more time to yourself, but the reality may be quite different. First there are off-season

Consider the fit

Athletic scholarships demand commitment

athletic duties that involve some form of participation—at a minimum, five days a week. In addition, your academic course load becomes much heavier to balance the lighter load you carried during the on-season."

Karen A., former Division I volleyball player, details her daily college schedule:

College sports are time-intensive

During Season	**Off Season**
7:30 am: weights	7:30 am: weights
9 am-3 pm: class/study	9 am-5 pm: class/study
4 pm: dinner	6-8 pm: practice
5-6 pm: break	
6:30 -9:30/10 pm: practice	
10 pm-midnight: study	

Jennifer P., a former Division I soccer player, shares a typical college day: "I'd usually wake up around 8:15 am, attend class from 9 till noon, work from noon to 2:30 pm, get taped, practice from 3 to 5:30, come home (finally!), shower, eat dinner, watch TV, then head out to study around 7:30 pm."

She adds, "You have to be very disciplined during the season, since you also have games twice a week and are traveling. In the off-season, we had weekends off, so we had a lot more time to ourselves."

Dominic S., former UCLA football player, describes his typical daily routine:

During Season	
8 am: wake up	3:30-5:30 pm: practice
9 am-noon: classes	5:45-6:45 pm: weights
noon-1 pm: lunch	6:45-7:15 pm: therapy/shower
1-2 pm: class	7:30 pm: dinner
2-2:30 pm: changing/therapy	8:30 pm: study
2:30-3:30 pm: pre-practice workout/meeting	12:30 am: bed

Coach Jane LaRiviere, Washington State University, discloses the schedule she assigns her women's rowing team:

During Season	**Off Season**
6:15-7:15 am MWF: lift weights	8 hrs. per week: lift weights and row
3:15-6 pm M-F: row on water	

In response to a question in our survey of former collegiate athletes— "What advice would you give to a high school student-athlete who wants to compete at the collegiate level?"— many athletes said they would have prepared themselves for the level of fitness they would be required to maintain when they got to college.

Mark S. advises, "You have to get yourself into the best condition of your life, in order to keep up with the much faster pace of the college game, as well as the increased physicality that comes from playing with and against people who are as much as four years older than yourself."

Mike L., former Division I varsity volleyball player, agrees: "The level of training is much higher in college than in high school. Remember, you are going to be competing against players who have played at the collegiate level for 1-4 years before you even arrived."

Learning to be a small fish in a big pond isn't easy. "An athlete must make the jump from being the star of his or her high school team to one of many in a college program. This is not a negative, but rather, is a requisite part of growing up," says Mark S.

In addition, the student-athlete needs to be prepared to make sacrifices. Jennifer P. warns, "For fall sports your summer break will be cut short for preseason training. For winter and spring sports, participants have to practice for an entire school year before getting to compete, and they often miss Thanksgiving, Christmas or spring break."

As you can see, participating in a competitive college sport is an adjustment for student-athletes and exacts many sacrifices. Besides learning to carefully balance their time, they are pressured to increase their skills and fitness to compete with others who are often older and more experienced, while having to adjust to a more regimented and professional sports atmosphere.

Dominick S. concurs: "Be prepared for college athletics to be as businesslike, political and bureaucratic as any professional corporation. This is not the sheltered sanctuary that high school may have been."

"Collegiate athletics is more like a job than a social activity," says Jennifer P.

However, even with these challenges, the overall experience of participating in collegiate athletics seems to be one most student-athletes would recommend. "I would participate in collegiate athletics again," states Ryan O., former Stanford volleyball player. "The discipline and work habits I developed in college have helped me in my personal and professional life, not to mention that I had a great time bonding with my teammates as we practiced and played together."

"The benefits and experiences you get by participating in collegiate athletics will, without question, be some of the greatest of your life," says Mike L.

Jennifer P. concludes: "Nothing can replace the strong friendships I made in my four years of college soccer. For that alone, I would do it again."

Whether or not to compete in collegiate athletics is a personal decision. Even after you have satisfied yourself that you have the athletic talent, you must still decide if the rewards justify the incredible sacrifices you will need to make. College athletics require a strong dedication, a desire to achieve and a drive to compete. Receiving an athletic scholarship can create additional pressure for you to perform. Make sure you want to participate because it will be a long, hard road if it is not something you truly want to do.

College athletics require strong dedication

Summary

⚽ Deciding whether you have the necessary potential to compete in your sport at the college level takes work.

⚽ Assessing yourself, compiling your statistics and seeking the opinions of others give you a strong indication of your potential to compete in collegiate sports.

⚽ Evaluating your athletic potential guides you in making the decision to go for a sports scholarship and lets you know in what areas you need to improve to be more competitive.

⚽ Learning what participation in college sports is really like gives you additional information to help you make an informed decision.

Although your athletic talent is key to winning a sports scholarship, there is another very important area to consider in assessing your college potential. Chapter 5 deals with the Big "A": Academics. ▌▌▌➡

5

How Athletics and Academics Go Hand in Hand

"If I were to give one piece of advice to quality prospective student-athletes, I would emphasize the importance of getting the best grades one can. There are a lot of very fine athletes competing for scholarships, and it often comes down to selecting the one who has the best grades because they will probably have the best chance of staying eligible through-out their entire collegiate career."

Chris Bates
Coach, men's lacrosse
Drexel University, Pennsylvania

It's Not Enough to Be a Skilled Athlete!

Scholastics + Sports = Sports Scholarship

Relying solely on your athletic ability won't win you a sports scholarship, but your chances multiply dramatically as your *grade point average (GPA)* increases. Colleges want students who have excelled in academics as well as in sports and who have shown motivation and self-discipline—the qualities necessary to be a successful college athlete and student.

Of course, there is no substitute for athletic ability; however, the combination of athletics and academics is unbeatable. "The talented athlete with good grades has it made," states high school coach Russ Peterich.

A solid academic background is impressive to college coaches, who have only so many scholarship dollars to offer incoming and continuing student-athletes. They cannot afford to allot these funds to athletes who are not self-disciplined academically or motivated in the classroom. They want students who can bring the same discipline to the playing field that they have to their studies.

Good Grades Can Make the Difference

Grades count!

The better student you are, the easier it is for a college coach to make a strong case for awarding you an athletic scholarship. "College coaches are better able to convince the athletic department and financial aid office to allocate precious scholarship dollars to high school students with good grades," claims Sam Koch, men's soccer coach, University of Massachusetts.

Colleges and universities want their students to graduate. Concern over the low graduation rate in some collegiate sports programs and the failure of a number of student-athletes to accumulate substantial academic *units* during their years at the university have put pressure on athletic departments to select the best student-athletes they can possibly recruit. They want to be satisfied that these recruits have the potential, as demonstrated by a proven track record, to graduate from their college.

For example, imagine that a college baseball coach who needs a pitcher with certain skills is recruiting from a list of ten candidates, including you, all with similar high school stats. All other factors being equal, the scholarship award will most likely go to the best student, the one with the highest potential to do well academically in college. You could very well be the one selected if you have a history of scholastic achievement.

"Anytime you have two recruits who have similar athletic abilities but one has a superior SAT and GPA…you have to go with that kid," says Cliff McCrath, men's soccer coach, Seattle Pacific University, Washington.

Athletes must keep up their grades to maintain eligibility and continue to play. A coach's worst nightmare is to lose a highly recruited diver or place kicker for a season because that athlete was placed on academic probation by the college and is ineligible to compete.

Although it is true that at some schools the admission requirements may be relaxed for the student-athlete, only so much leeway can be allowed, and it is usually allotted to the most talented and the most highly recruited prospects. Although it is possible that a coach will go to bat for you in admissions, you cannot afford to expect this treatment. Remember: If you cannot get admitted to the college based on your academic record, it doesn't matter how talented you are as an athlete. By getting good grades, you will position yourself as a strong candidate for admission to college on your own, without having to hope for assistance from a coach.

Beth Anders, field hockey coach, Old Dominion University in Virginia, says, "There are three main factors I look for in a prospective recruit…1) academic ability, 2) athletic ability and 3) a strong desire to be part of our program."

So, just as you practice your sport and work out to increase your athletic skills, you must prepare yourself academically while in high school. For most colleges, your grade point average, *class standing* and your *SAT (Scholastic Aptitude Test)* and/or *ACT (American College Test)* scores are carefully reviewed when you are under consideration for admission, as well as for a scholarship.

GPA (Grade Point Average)

According to the NCAA, GPA is based on the values of grades earned in your *core courses* as measured by a common scale, typically, a four-point scale.

A = 4 points   B = 3 points   C = 2 points   D = 1 point

Class Standing or Rank

Class standing or class rank is an indication of your academic placement relative to other students in the same grade at your high school, generally measured by a student's GPA. For example: Your GPA may place you number 20 out of 300 total students in your class, ranking you in the top 10 percent (20/300 = 6.7 percent).

SAT/ACT

Take your SATs

The SAT is required by some colleges for admission, while the ACT is required by others. Many schools will accept either test, but you need to check with individual institutions for their requirements. Obviously, as far as your chances for admissions are concerned, the higher you score the better. In fact, in our College Recruiting Survey, 91 percent of college coaches surveyed considered standardized test scores (either the SAT or ACT) to be extremely important data in evaluating a recruit. It's best to take either or both tests for the first time early in your junior year so you will have time to retake them if your score is not high enough to get into a particular school. Students from the seventh grade on up can take preliminary versions of each test for preparation purposes.

SAT Subject Tests

Some colleges require that you submit not only the SAT or ACT but also *SAT Subject Tests* results, which are designed to measure your knowledge and skills in particular subjects. Ask your guidance counselor for more information about the SAT Subject Tests, and check with colleges you are interested in to see if they require them.

Even if the institution does not require that you take the SAT or ACT, both the NCAA and NAIA, the two largest athletic associations, require athletes playing collegiate sports to take and obtain a minimum score on either test.

Academic Planning

The process of getting into the college of your choice begins as early as the ninth grade and continues on through high school. Taking the appropriate classes each year—and doing your best in them—should all be part of your plan to go to college. Your guidance counselor knows which classes you need to satisfy college entrance requirements and can set up a four-year plan with you to reach your goals. If you have not talked to your counselor regarding pre-college planning, do so right away. Or you might consult with a professional college admissions counselor, sometimes called an independent educational consultant.

Academic Eligibility Requirements

Make sure you take core courses

Student-athletes who want to participate in collegiate athletics need to be aware that there are strict academic regulations for high school students. The rules are ever-changing and often confusing. We have summarized all of the important ones here, but you should check with the NCAA for the current eligibility rules.

According to NCAA regulations, incoming college student-athletes must have fulfilled specific core courses in high school to practice and play their sport at an NCAA Division I or Division II college during their freshman year. They must also have achieved a minimum combination of GPA and standardized test scores.

"A 'core course'," as stated in the 2006-07 *NCAA Guide for the College-Bound Student-Athlete,* "is defined as a recognized academic course (as opposed to a vocational or personal-services course) that offers fundamental instructional components in a specified area of study; courses that are taught at a level below the high school's regular academic instructional level (e.g., remedial, special education or compensatory) cannot be considered core courses regardless of course content."

For more in-depth information about core curriculum and changes in NCAA regulations that might affect you, read the *NCAA Guide for the College-Bound Student-Athlete,* which is updated annually and available in your counselor's office or by contacting NCAA. The NAIA, NJCAA and other athletic associations have regulations that may differ from those of the NCAA. Again, ask your counselor for information or contact the athletic associations directly. See the Resources list on page 156.

NCAA Initial Eligibility Clearinghouse

If you wish to participate in NCAA Division I or Division II sports, **you must be certified by the NCAA *Initial Eligibility Clearinghouse (IEC).*** Established in 1993 by the NCAA and implemented by the American College Testing Program, the IEC is designed to determine academic eligibility of student-athletes. This is done by comparing high school academic records and SAT or ACT test scores with NCAA eligibility requirements (see Table 4, page 34) and certifying to colleges whether you meet all requirements.

If you are planning to play sports at an institution that is not a member of the NCAA, you will need to be certified as academically eligible by that school. Only NCAA member colleges and universities are affiliated with the IEC.

An advantage of the IEC to the student-athlete is that it provides a consistent one-source evaluation of academic eligibility. Additionally, you need to send your academic records to one source, not to every NCAA institution you are interested in attending.

You have to pay a registration fee ($50 for domestic and $75 for international students), although under certain circumstances, you may be eligible for a fee waiver. See your high school guidance counselor for more details and to get your information packet and the forms you need, or contact the NCAA Initial Eligibility Clearinghouse at P.O. Box 4043, Iowa City, Iowa 52243-4043. You can also phone (877) 262-1492 or visit the website at www.ncaaclearinghouse.net and can sign up on the website.

The NCAA advises student-athletes to begin the certification process at the end of their junior year of high school. Preliminary certification is based on information available before graduation, while final certification is based on preliminary information plus proof of graduation (final transcripts.) When you take the SAT/ACT, mark the appropriate box for the IEC so your scores will be sent directly from the testing service. Otherwise, you will receive your scores and must then send them to the IEC yourself.

Starting with the college class beginning its freshman year in 2007, the IEC has added a process for determining the amateur status of student-athletes. According to Dan Colandro, NCAA member services assistant director, "There is a series of questions for the student-athlete to answer as part of the online application to help determine whether he or she is eligible to compete as an amateur."

The NCAA Division I and II eligibility requirements are given in Table 4, page 34. Division III does not use the NCAA Initial-Eligibility Clearinghouse. Contact your Division III college regarding its policies on financial aid, practice and competition.

Register with the NCAA Initial Eligibility Clearinghouse

TABLE 4:
NCAA COLLEGE ELIGIBILITY REQUIREMENTS

Division I Between 2005 and 2007

If you enroll in a Division I college between 2005 and 2007 and want to participate in athletics or receive an athletics scholarship during your first year, you must:

➤ Graduate from high school;
➤ Complete these 14 core courses:
>   4 years of English
>   2 years of math (algebra 1 or higher)
>   2 years of natural or physical science (including one year of lab science if offered by your high school)
>   1 extra year of English, math or natural or physical science
>   2 years of social science
>   3 years of extra core courses (from any category above, or foreign language, nondoctrinal religion or philosophy);
➤ Earn a minimum required grade-point average in your core courses; and
➤ Earn a combined SAT or ACT sum score that matches your core-course grade-point average and test score sliding scale (see Division I Core GPA and Test Score Sliding Scale). For example, a 2.400 core-course grade-point average needs an 860 SAT.

Note: Computer science courses can be used as core courses only if your high school grants graduation credit in math or natural or physical science for them, and if the courses appear on your high school's core-course list as a math or science course.

You will be a _qualifier_ if you meet the academic requirements listed above. As a qualifier, you:

➤ Can practice or compete for your college or university during your first year of college;
➤ Can receive an athletics scholarship during your first year of college; and
➤ Can play four seasons in your sport as long as you maintain your eligibility from year to year.

You will be a _nonqualifier_ if you do not meet the academic requirements listed above. As a nonqualifier, you:

➤ Cannot practice or compete for your college or university during your first year of college;
➤ Cannot receive an athletics scholarship during your first year of college, although you may receive need-based financial aid; and
➤ Can play only three seasons in your sport as long as you maintain your eligibility from year to year (to earn a fourth season you must complete at least 80 percent of your degree before beginning your fifth year of college).

Division I 2008 and Later

If you enroll in a Division I college in 2008 or later and want to participate in athletics or receive an athletics scholarship during your first year, you must:

➤ Graduate from high school;
➤ Complete these 16 core courses:
>   4 years of English
>   3 years of math (algebra 1 or higher)
>   2 years of natural or physical science (including one year of lab science if offered by your high school)
>   1 extra year of English, math or natural or physical science
>   2 years of social science
>   4 years of extra core courses (from any category above, or foreign language, nondoctrinal religion or philosophy);
➤ Earn a minimum required grade-point average in your core courses; and
➤ Earn a combined SAT or ACT sum score that matches your core-course grade-point average and test score sliding scale (see Division I Core GPA and Test Score Sliding Scale). For example, a 2.400 core-course grade-point average needs an 860 SAT.

Note: Computer science courses can be used as core courses only if your high school grants graduation credit in math or natural or physical science for them, and if the courses appear on your high school's core-course list as a math or science course.

Division II 2005 and Later

If you enroll in a Division II college in 2005 or later and want to participate in athletics or receive an athletics scholarship during your first year, you must:

➢ Graduate from high school;

➢ Complete these 14 core courses:

> 3 years of English
> 2 years of math (algebra 1 or higher)
> 2 years of natural or physical science (including one year of lab science if offered by your high school)
> 2 extra years of English, math or natural or physical science
> 2 years of social science
> 3 years of extra core courses (from any category above, or foreign language, nondoctrinal religion or philosophy);

➢ Earn a 2.000 grade-point average or better in your core courses; and

➢ Earn a combined SAT score of 820 or an ACT sum score of 68. There is no sliding scale in Division II.

Note: Computer science courses can be used as core courses only if your high school grants graduation credit in math or natural or physical science for them, and if the courses appear on your high school's core-course list as a math or science course.

You will be a qualifier if you meet the academic requirements listed above. As a qualifier you:

➢ Can practice or compete for your college or university during your first year of college;

➢ Can receive an athletic scholarship during your first year of college; and

➢ Can play four seasons in your sport as long as you maintain your eligibility from year to year.

You will be a *partial qualifier* if you do not meet all of the academic requirements listed above but you have graduated from high school and meet one of the following:

➢ The combined SAT score of 820 or ACT sum score of 68; or

➢ Completion of the 14 core courses with a 2.000 core-course grade-point average.

As a partial qualifier, you:

➢ Can practice with your team at its home facility during your first year of college;

➢ Can receive an athletics scholarship during your first year of college;

➢ Cannot compete during your first year of college; and

➢ Can play four seasons in your sport as long as you maintain your eligibility from year to year.

You will be a nonqualifier if you did not graduate from high school, or if you graduated and are missing both the core-course grade-point average or the required ACT or SAT scores. As a nonqualifier, you:

➢ Cannot practice or compete for your college or university during your first year of college;

➢ Cannot receive an athletics scholarship during your first year of college, although you may receive need-based financial aid; and

➢ Can play four seasons in your sport as long as you maintain your eligibility from year to year.

TABLE 5:
MINIMUM REQUIREMENTS FOR
NCAA DIVISION I ELIGIBILITY

Division I Core GPA and Test Score Sliding Scale

Core GPA	SAT	ACT	Core GPA	SAT	ACT
3.550 & above	400	37	2.750	720	59
3.525	410	38	2.725	730	59
3.500	420	39	2.700	730	60
3.475	430	40	2.675	740-750	61
3.450	440	41	2.650	760	62
3.425	450	41	2.625	770	63
3.400	460	42	2.600	780	64
3.375	470	42	2.575	790	65
3.350	480	43	2.550	800	66
3.325	490	44	2.525	810	67
3.300	500	44	2.500	820	68
3.275	510	45	2.475	830	69
3.250	520	46	2.450	840-850	70
3.225	530	46	2.425	860	70
3.200	540	47	2.400	860	71
3.175	550	47	2.375	870	72
3.150	560	48	2.350	880	73
3.125	570	49	2.325	890	74
3.100	580	49	2.300	900	75
3.075	590	50	2.275	910	76
3.050	600	50	2.250	920	77
3.025	610	51	2.225	930	78
3.000	620	52	2.200	940	79
2.975	630	52	2.175	950	80
2.950	640	53	2.150	960	80
2.925	650	53	2.125	960	81
2.900	660	54	2.100	970	82
2.875	670	55	2.075	980	83
2.850	680	56	2.050	990	84
2.825	690	56	2.025	1000	85
2.800	700	57	2.000	1010	86
2.775	710	58			

2006-07 NCAA Guide for the College-Bound Student-Athlete

How to Win a Sports Scholarship

Academic Self-Assessment

Just as you earlier assessed your college athletic potential, you should also assess your academic preparedness for college. In your quest to understand where you fit in athletically, you asked your coaches to help you assess your strengths and weaknesses. Now you should talk to people familiar with your scholastic record to determine whether you have met or are on track to meet academic requirements and deadlines. The following three steps will help you gain a realistic picture of your academic progress and standing:

Look at your academics

- Compile and compare your academic statistics.
- Assess yourself.
- Seek the advice of others.

Compile and Compare Your Academic Statistics

To measure yourself against other student-athletes, you needed to gather your athletic statistics. You should do the same for academics. Stats you need to look at include your GPA, SAT/ACT and other test scores, plus class standing or rank. These will give you an indication of where you stand in comparison to others, as well as show you areas in which you need improvement to satisfy applicable minimum college requirements.

Depending on your grade level, these statistics may not yet be available. For example, if you are a sophomore and have not taken the SAT/ACT yet, look at your preliminary test scores to get an indication of where you stand. A comparison of your scores relative to the average scores of others taking the test will be provided on the report included with your test scores.

To establish your class standing or rank, see your guidance counselor or visit the registrar's office at your high school, providing your school compiles and releases such information. Compiling your academic stats early will help in planning ahead.

Answering the following questions will help assess your academic progress and standing. For the younger high school student, your responses will help you plan ahead. For the older student, they indicate whether you have met the minimum requirements and are on track for admission to a four-year college.

ACADEMIC SELF-ASSESSMENT QUIZ

1. Am I planning to take or have I taken all of the necessary core-curriculum courses at my school (see Table 4 on pages 34 and 35 for specific requirements). Have I successfully completed them?

	Years	Course Name
English	1	_____
	2	_____
	3	_____
	4	_____
Mathematics	1	_____
	2	_____
	3	_____
Natural or physical science	1	_____
	2	_____
Social science	1	_____
	2	_____
Additional core courses	1	_____
	2	_____
	3	_____
	4	_____
	5	_____

2. What is my core-curriculum course GPA? _____

3. Does my GPA in the core-curriculum courses meet the minimum eligibility requirements for participating in college sports? _____

4. Am I planning to take or have I taken the necessary standardized tests (PSAT, SAT, ACT)?

	Date Taken	Score	Date Retaken	Score
PSAT	_____	_____	_____	_____
SAT	_____	_____	_____	_____
ACT	_____	_____	_____	_____

5. Do these scores meet at least the minimum eligibility requirements? _____

6. Am I planning to take or have I taken any necessary achievement tests?

Name of Test	Date Taken	Score
_____	_____	_____
_____	_____	_____
_____	_____	_____

7. What is my overall GPA? _____

8. Is my overall GPA above average? _____

9. How does my overall GPA compare to the GPAs of other students in my grade?

What is my class standing? _____

What percentile does this place me in? _____

10. Am I taking the highest level of courses that I feel I can handle at my school? _____

11. Am I taking or have I taken all of the necessary courses to meet my high school's graduation requirements? _____

12. Do I feel I would succeed if I increase both my academic course load and the amount of time devoted to athletics? _____

13. Do I work hard inside and outside the classroom to correct those areas in which I need improvement? _____

14. Am I competitive in the classroom? _____

15. At what level of college academics would I be at my best? (check one)

highly competitive? _____ challenging? _____

moderately competitive? _____ ungraded? _____

16. If I were a college admissions officer looking at my grades and tests scores, would I admit myself to college? If not, what do I need to do to improve my chances for admission?

Talk to the academic experts

If your answers to these questions are mostly yes, you are probably on track for admission to a four-year college program and for meeting minimum requirements. You should also compare your answers with the NCAA eligibility requirements on page 36. Other intercollegiate athletic associations have similar requirements, but you should check with individual schools as to their eligibility criteria.

In some cases, not all of the preceding questions may apply to your particular situation. For example, students who may be considering community colleges as an option or other alternatives to four-year schools may face different requirements. More about community colleges and other alternatives is found in Chapter 7.

What if you have taken the quiz and your academic potential is not looking so promising? If you are reading this book early enough in your high school career you have time to turn over a new leaf academically, or if you are already an accomplished student, keep up the good work!

Seek The Advice Of Others

You come into contact with many people in your academic life who can advise and assist you. Enlist the support of these people to help you gain additional insight into your chances for college success.

Guidance counselor

One of the most important people to help you assess your academic potential is your school guidance counselor. Your counselor's opinion of your academic skills is as valuable as your coach's opinion of your athletic skills. He or she can help you plan your entire high school schedule so that you meet all the necessary requirements and can follow up on your progress, making sure that you are on track. Your counselor can also help with academic advice and problem-solving. The following story serves as an example:

A North Carolina high school student-athlete had his heart set on playing tennis at a highly competitive east coast university. He took the SAT twice but each time failed to score well. He asked his counselor if she thought he should try it again. She suggested he take the ACT instead because she felt he might do better on it than on the SAT. While the SAT is based on two areas, namely math and English, the ACT has four components—English, mathematics, reading (which focuses on social studies/sciences and arts/literature) and science. The student's intense interest in both history and science led him to ace the reading and science reasoning sections, while he stayed at pretty much the same level in English and math. Therefore, his overall score on the ACT was considerably higher than on the SAT, and the school he wanted to attend accepted either score. His high school counselor, by offering that one piece of advice, may have made the difference in his being accepted to the school of his choice.

Other counselors

Some high schools and most college and public libraries have an area or a counseling center where you can conduct research about colleges and universities. Usually, there are computers for researching plus numerous resource books, brochures and catalogs about individual colleges. This is a good way to help you start thinking about the schools for which you might qualify. Make sure any print or online information you use is current.

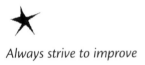

Always strive to improve

Professional college admissions counselors (sometimes called independent educational consultants) are another resource for students and their parents. The need for independent consultants in the college admissions field has grown out of economic cutbacks. These budget cuts have resulted in a decrease in the ratio of counselors to students, leaving scant time in some cases for the counselor to address individual student needs.

To find an independent educational consultant, ask in your high school counseling office and check the online directories of the Higher Education Consultants Association (www.hecaonline.org) and the National Association of College Admissions (www.nacacnet.org). You can also conduct an online search using the keywords "college counselor."

Parents, teachers and others

People you may also want to consult are your parents, teachers and others who are knowledgeable in the academic arena and, above all, interested in you and your future. Of these, your parents are probably your most valuable source of support, and your communication with them should be ongoing. The fact is, they have a vested interest in what you do, knowledge to share and assistance to offer, so view them as a resource. Your parents can be your best allies as you plan for the future.

A favorite teacher, relative or mentor can also provide input about your potential for collegiate success. Any adult who knows you well and has watched you perform either in the classroom, on the job or in other areas is in a good position to critique your strengths, suggest ways to correct the areas that need improvement and generally offer encouragement and support.

Putting It All Together

If you have evaluated the information you gathered about yourself and found you are on track academically, congratulations! And if the results from your athletic assessment also are positive, you may be on your way to winning a sports scholarship.

But what if you discover that you haven't planned well or have goofed off, studying little and barely getting by? First of all, if it is early in your high school career, you can change your ways. Again, talk to your guidance counselor to find out how you can improve your grades. A change of attitude may be the most important factor, along with your commitment to study more. But you may also benefit by learning better study habits and improving your time-management skills. The following suggestions might help.

Improving Your Grades

There are many ways to help improve your grades. High schools sometimes offer study skills workshops, as well as tutorial services. Additionally, talking with your classroom teachers may provide excellent suggestions on what you can do to improve in their classes. Often, suggestions from one teacher can assist you in all of your classes.

"Read a book on the subject of how to improve your grades," says Regan Ronayne, M.A., professional college admissions counselor in California. "One of my favorites is *Becoming a Master Student,* by Dave Campbell."

Summer school programs are another alternative. Summer school enables you to make up classes you failed or barely passed and to take classes you may need for your core-curriculum requirements. Unfortunately, attending summer school can also cause scheduling conflicts because summer is a prime time for honing your athletic skills in summer leagues and attending sports camps. But remember, if you can't get admitted to college based on your academic record, you will miss out on the opportunity to play collegiate sports anyway.

Your high school may be able to recommend a local tutoring service or a private tutor to help you catch up or enhance your learning skills. Private schools and learning centers may also offer tutoring, for a fee, in areas where you need remediation. These schools or centers may also give classes for SAT/ACT test-taking preparation.

Whatever you feel you can do to improve your grades, as long as it is ethical, is worth the effort. And, of course, if it means the difference between receiving a scholarship and not, it is worth its weight in gold!

10 Tips to Increase Your GPA and Improve Your Study Habits

1. Study harder.
2. Study longer.
3. Don't wait until the last minute to study.
4. Improve your time-management skills.
5. Attend study skills workshops.
6. Hire a tutor (or trade services).
7. Ask your teachers for extra help.
8. Study with a friend; form study groups.
9. Attend summer school.
10. Take an intensive course at a commercial learning center.

Going that extra mile to improve your grades can mean the difference between your receiving a scholarship and losing out!

But what if you are already a senior who concentrated on your sport but ignored academics? There's still hope. Although your chances might not be as good as someone of equal talent with better grades, you may get a college coach to go to bat for you in the admissions office and help you get admitted. More on recruiting rules is found in Chapter 11.

Another alternative is the two-year community college. More on community colleges and other alternatives is found in Chapter 7.

Summary

⚽   Being a skilled athlete is not enough; college coaches look for student-athletes with a proven academic track record.

⚽   Student-athletes must meet minimum academic requirements to compete in a college sport.

⚽   The NCAA Initial Eligibility Clearinghouse certifies the academic eligibility of student-athletes, as well as their amateur status. All athletes who want to play their sport at an NCAA Division I or II college must be certified by the IEC.

⚽   Assessing your scholastic aptitude and high school achievements will help you decide whether you have the potential for academic success in college.

⚽   Your guidance counselor can help you plan ahead so that you meet the necessary requirements.

⚽   If you need academic assistance, there are many things you can do to improve your study habits, GPA and test scores.

⚽   It is your responsibility to seek out the people and resources that can best help you.

By now you should have a pretty good idea of whether you are on track for going to college and competing in a collegiate sports program. Chapter 6 introduces you to the steps for getting started on your quest for a sports scholarship. ▮▮➡

6

The Process Begins

"The way to get my attention is to write or e-mail directly. We will then begin gathering important data on grades, experience and other interests and start determining at what events we can see the athlete in action."

Shellie Onstead
Coach, field hockey
University of California, Berkeley

Develop your Game Plan

The game plan is your marketing strategy for grabbing the attention of coaches whose college academic and athletic programs might best suit your needs and talents.

Just as a coach develops an overall strategy for the upcoming season to position a team to win the championship, you need to develop a game plan to increase your chances of winning a sports scholarship. Your game plan should reflect your goals and objectives and a schedule for meeting them. In chapters 6, 7 and 8 we will walk you through our proven game plan and show you just what to do.

The recruiting process is ongoing. Although the entire process can be squeezed into a relatively short period of time, ideally it will begin early in your high school years. Regardless of when you start, you will want to follow the process outlined below in order to reach your goals.

Showcase your talent

Throughout the process you will be collecting athletic and academic information about yourself as well as compiling your statistics so that you can provide them to college coaches. You need to create a system to organize this information and correspondence that colleges send you in response to your initial contact letter, which will be discussed in Chapter 7.

You will be developing your own *Sports Resume Kit*, which will showcase your talents in a concise, easy-to-read format. You will be investigating colleges and athletic programs to send it to. You will continue to compete in your sport and improve your skills while maintaining good grades, taking your SAT/ACT tests, applying to colleges and considering *scholarship offers.*

Planning and Keeping Track

A timeline and checklist helps you visualize, plan and keep track of what you need to do to achieve your goals. Some of the tasks listed are ongoing, and some you have already completed. The Planning Checklist and Timeline at a Glance (see pages 47–50) will help you reach your goals, which are three-fold:

- Gain acceptance to the college that can provide you the best education possible
- Participate in your sport at the collegiate level
- Win a sports scholarship

Because the recruiting process is ongoing, you will work on many of the tasks listed more than once, and you will often be focusing on several at a time. For instance, you will continue to document your awards, compile and create new statistics, strive to play at the highest levels possible and have yourself videotaped in competition. You will find that as you become interested in colleges, you will be requesting information at various times throughout the process and communicating with college coaches. Therefore, at any given time you will be at different stages of the recruiting process with each school you contact.

Plan for success

Use the following Planning Checklist throughout your high school career to help you stay on task.

PLANNING CHECKLIST

Freshman/Sophomore Years   Year:_____

Academic tasks to do

- ❏ Meet with guidance counselor to create a 4-year academic plan to satisfy core-course and college entrance requirements.
- ❏ Take the PSAT.
- ❏ Calculate Grade Point Average (GPA) and determine class rank, if possible.
- ❏ Take Academic Self-Assessment Quiz on pages 38 and 39. Improve study habits, if necessary.
- ❏ Begin researching colleges that complement your academic abilities and career goals by browsing college guides and college websites. See Resources list on page 163.
- ❏ Begin saving newspaper articles, awards or other recognition of your scholastic performance.

Athletic tasks to do

- ❏ Take Athletic Self-Assessment Quiz on page 21. Determine areas that need improvement and focus on those areas.
- ❏ Communicate your desire to participate in your sport at the collegiate level to coaches and other people who might help you.
- ❏ Begin saving newspaper articles, awards or other recognition of your athletic achievements.
- ❏ Create a filing system to keep the information and correspondence you receive from coaches and colleges.
- ❏ Seek the advice of others regarding your athletic potential and convey your willingness to strengthen any weak areas. People to contact include your coach, coaches from opposing teams and those associated with college athletics.
- ❏ Put together a team of people who will help you reach your goals. This team may include parents, coaches, counselors, teachers and other mentors.
- ❏ Find a current or former college athlete and ask questions about the realities of college athletics and your potential future as a college athlete.
- ❏ Review the NCAA recruiting rules to prevent yourself from unknowingly becoming a victim of illegal recruiting practices.
- ❏ Send initial contact letters or e-mails to the coaches at schools from which you want more information.
- ❏ Promptly fill out and return all player profile sheets you receive from college coaches or access online.
- ❏ Compete at the highest levels possible for maximum exposure, such as on all-star teams and in high-profile athletic contests.
- ❏ Arrange for videotaping of your athletic contests, so you will have footage of yourself in action if a coach requests it.
- ❏ Attend holiday/summer sports camps, if possible.

Notes:_____

_____

Junior Year or Earlier

Academic tasks to do

- ❏ Obtain the current *NCAA Guide for the College-Bound Student-Athlete*.
- ❏ Take the SAT and/or ACT. Be sure to forward your scores to the NCAA Initial Eligibility Clearinghouse. See page 34.
- ❏ Calculate your current GPA and determine your class rank, if possible.
- ❏ Retake Academic Self-Assessment Quiz on pages 38 and 39 to ensure that you are meeting your academic goals and to set new ones.
- ❏ Research print and internet college guides and pick a maximum of 30 schools that interest you and reflect your general academic criteria.
- ❏ Request general information about these schools from their admissions office or get from their websites.
- ❏ If you have not already done so, create a filing system for organizing your information.
- ❏ Save articles and other evidence of your academic achievements.

Athletic tasks to do

- ❏ Register with the NCAA Initial Eligibility Clearinghouse (junior year).
- ❏ Retake Athletic Self-Assessment Quiz on page 21 to ensure that you are still on the right path.
- ❏ Research athletic programs through print or website guides; see Resources list on page 163 and identify college programs that offer scholarships in your sport. Cross-check these schools with the ones you selected according to general academic criteria. Make a list of the schools that satisfy both your academic and athletic requirements.
- ❏ Narrow the number of schools on your list to only those whose athletic level is near your own, for example Division I, II, III.
- ❏ Mail or e-mail initial contact letters to the coaches at schools from which you want more information.
- ❏ Fill out and promptly return all player profile sheets you receive from college coaches.
- ❏ Continue to save articles and awards about your athletic achievements.
- ❏ Ask individuals who are knowledgeable about your athletic talent to write letters of recommendation. See pages 91-93.
- ❏ Assemble your Sports Resume Kit. See Chapter 8.
- ❏ Send your Sports Resume Kit to coaches at schools that interest you.
- ❏ Follow-up on your Sports Resume Kit (about two weeks later) with phone calls or e-mails to coaches to show interest.
- ❏ Send videotapes/DVDs of yourself to coaches, if applicable.
- ❏ Attend holiday/summer sports camps, if possible.
- ❏ Continue to compete at the highest levels possible for maximum exposure, such as on all-star teams and in high-profile athletic contests.

Notes: _____

_____

_____

Senior Year or Earlier

Academic tasks to do

❏ Obtain current *NCAA Guide for the College-Bound Student-Athlete.*
❏ Re-take the SAT/ACT, if necessary.
❏ Narrow your college choices to those you are truly interested in, based on the combination of academic and athletic opportunities they offer. Use the College Rating Sheet on page 161.
❏ Send your SAT/ACT scores to these schools if you or the SAT/ACT has not already done so.
❏ Visit the campuses of your top college choices.
❏ Apply to colleges.
❏ Apply for financial aid at those schools, if applicable.
❏ After receiving your acceptances of admission, select the school you wish to attend.
❏ Maintain grades throughout your senior year.

Athletic tasks to do

❏ Review recruiting rules in the current *NCAA Guide for the College-Bound Student-Athlete.*
❏ Inform college coaches of your continuing interest in their program.
❏ Take recruiting trips to the schools you are most interested in.
❏ Send videotapes/DVDs to coaches, if applicable.
❏ Negotiate scholarship offers, if applicable.
❏ Sign a letter of intent, if applicable.
❏ Stay in shape for upcoming college season.
❏ Continue to improve your athletic skills.

Notes: _____

_____

_____

_____

_____

_____

_____

_____

_____

_____

TIMELINE AT A GLANCE

Frosh/Soph Years

Academic:

- ❏ Meet with guidance counselor
- ❏ Take the PSAT
- ❏ Calculate GPA and determine class rank, if possible
- ❏ Take Academic Self-Assessment Quiz
- ❏ Obtain current *NCAA Guide for the College-Bound Student Athlete*
- ❏ Begin researching colleges
- ❏ Save articles and awards for academic achievement

Athletic:

- ❏ Take Athletic Self-Assessment Quiz
- ❏ Announce your desire to participate in collegiate sports
- ❏ Create a filing system
- ❏ Save athletic articles and awards
- ❏ Seek the advice of coaches and others
- ❏ Talk to college athletes
- ❏ Begin gathering your support team
- ❏ Begin researching athletic programs
- ❏ Learn recruiting rules
- ❏ Send initial contact letter via mail or e-mail
- ❏ Return player profile sheets
- ❏ Compete at the highest levels
- ❏ Videotape athletic contests
- ❏ Attend holiday/summer sports camps

Junior Year

Academic:

- ❏ Obtain current *NCAA Guide for the College-Bound Student Athlete*
- ❏ Take the SAT/ACT
- ❏ Calculate GPA and determine your class rank, if possible
- ❏ Retake Academic Self-Assessment Quiz
- ❏ Choose a maximum of 30 colleges that interest you
- ❏ Request information from those colleges
- ❏ Continue to save articles and awards

Athletic:

- ❏ Register with NCAA Initial Eligibility Clearinghouse
- ❏ Retake Athletic Self-Assessment Quiz
- ❏ Research and select athletic programs that interest you
- ❏ Send initial contact letters to coaches
- ❏ Return player profile sheets you receive or download from college website
- ❏ Continue to save athletic articles and awards
- ❏ Request letters of recommendation
- ❏ Assemble and send Sports Resume Kit
- ❏ Follow-up with phone calls or e-mails to coaches
- ❏ Videotape athletic contests
- ❏ Compete at the highest levels
- ❏ Send videotapes, if applicable
- ❏ Attend holiday/summer sports camps
- ❏ Update college coaches, as necessary

Senior Year

Academic:

- ❏ Retake the SAT/ACT, if necessary
- ❏ Narrow college choices
- ❏ Visit campuses
- ❏ Apply to colleges
- ❏ Apply for financial aid
- ❏ Review admission acceptance(s)
- ❏ Select school
- ❏ Maintain grades throughout senior year

Athletic:

- ❏ Review recruiting rules in current *NCAA Guide for the College-Bound Student Athlete*
- ❏ Update college coaches, as necessary
- ❏ Take recruiting trips
- ❏ Send videotapes or DVDs, if applicable
- ❏ Negotiate scholarship offers, if applicable
- ❏ Sign a letter of intent, if applicable
- ❏ Stay in shape for upcoming college season
- ❏ Continue to improve athletic skills

The Importance Of Starting Early

Ideally, your freshman or sophomore years of high school are the best times to start the process, at least to begin thinking about participating in collegiate athletics and gathering information. But if you are a junior or even a senior, it's OK. You will just have to condense the process into a shorter period of time. The important thing is to get the ball rolling. So, **start now!**

Selecting Your Team

Without help in the recruiting process, you may find it overwhelming, as there is too much for one person to do. But there is an answer: Teamwork. Think of the recruiting process as a team effort, rather than an individual sport. Just as you would choose the best players around you to make up a sports team, you need to gather the best people available to help you choose a college and win a sports scholarship.

Choose your teammates

Teammates are vital to your success. They can act as consultants, giving you valuable information about specific college sports programs and coaching personnel, and as guides, helping you wind your way through a sometimes complicated search for the right school. They can also speak on your behalf, recommending you to college coaches as a person of good character and a superior student-athlete. More on *recommendations* is found on pages 91-93.

You probably talked to many of your "teammates" when you asked your coaches and counselors for an assessment of your athletic and academic abilities. But, there are other people you will want to recruit at this stage.

The following list includes some of the potential key members of your team. Although not all of them may be available to help you or even appropriate to your situation, seek out and contact these people, and ask them to be part of your team.

YOUR ALL-STAR TEAM

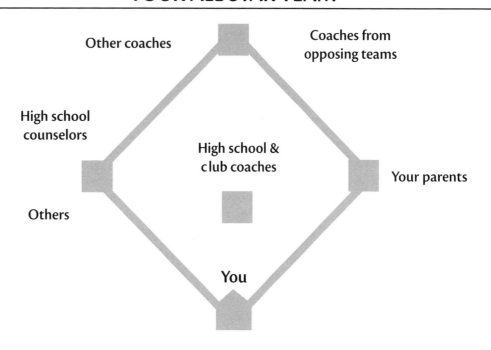

You, the Student-Athlete

Every team needs a leader, and because you are the one with the most at stake, you are the team captain. However, you are also the coach and offensive coordinator. You must select and gather your players and communicate your goals to them effectively, so that every member of your team knows what he or she is expected to do. Sound like a lot of work? Well, that's another reason you need a team: to help you with an important project that involves considerable time and effort.

Your Parents

Your parents can be your most effective co-captains. They need to be involved in the process as early as possible. Not only are they closest to you, but there are many factors to consider when selecting a college, and some factors, such as finances, may directly affect your parents.

David D. Cuttino, longtime dean of undergraduate admissions at Tufts University in Medford, Massachusetts, counsels high school students: "Pursuing a college education, like pursuing anything of value in life, requires its share of personal and financial sacrifice. You and your parents will have to weigh the value of personal and intellectual growth that comes with higher education against the financial cost that you will bear over the next four years and, for most students who require financial aid, beyond."

So talk to your parents. Include them in your thoughts and plans from the earliest stages. Keep them involved and tap into their experience. Ask them what they think and consider their suggestions. Your parents will be your main advocates and your trusted advisors throughout the process.

Your High School and Club Coaches

Your high school and club coaches can be tremendous resources for you because they know your skills and talents better than anyone else. They may have been associated with you for years and had the opportunity to watch you grow and mature. They know your strengths and can help you work on areas that need improvement.

Your high school and club coaches are often familiar with various colleges and can point you in the direction of schools with programs to fit your abilities and goals. They may be in contact with college coaches and recruiters and can let them know about you. In the recruiting process, college coaches generally talk to a student-athlete's high school and/or club coach when determining sports potential, so even if your coach can't offer you specific advice or helpful introductions, having his or her support and recommendation is key.

John Ross, women's basketball and men's tennis coach, Calvin College, Michigan, has this recommendation: "Have the high school coach do as much work as possible to help you find a school that matches your academic needs and athletic abilities."

Coaches are often involved with many athletes at a time, so never assume that they know your plans or can anticipate your needs. Besides, coaches have numerous other responsibilities. Make sure you contact them early in the process so they can give you the necessary attention. Many on-campus high school coaches teach physical education and other subjects and may coach more than one sport. Off-campus coaches, who might be employed elsewhere and come to your school only to coach, have even less contact with students off the practice field and limited time to spend on the needs of athletes while at school. It is your responsibility to tell your coaches as early as possible that you want to compete in your sport in college and are trying to get a sports scholarship. Let them know you need their support.

Coaches from Opposing Teams

Coaches are your allies

Opposing team coaches are an often untapped resource for athletes. They have probably already assessed your skills to play effectively against your team and have the advantage of having observed you play. Opposing coaches can write *letters of recommendation* that add strength to your sports resume and can talk to college coaches on your behalf. Getting an opposing coach on your team gives you another valuable advocate. See Chapter 8, page 93, for a sample letter of recommendation from an opposing coach.

Other Coaches

Attending sport camps can help you in several ways. Besides learning new skills and techniques, you also profit from different coaching and increased playing and practice time. Sports camp coaches can be excellent sources of recommendations. If a camp is run by high school coaches, they can recommend you to college coaches when you get to the recruiting stage. If the camp is associated with a college, camp coaches know what college coaches look for in a student-athlete and can suggest ways to improve your chances of being recruited. Additionally, they may be in the position of recruiting you themselves one day.

High School Counselors

Guidance counselors

Meet with your counselor

Your guidance counselor can be an invaluable member of your team. He or she can guide you through the academic maze, helping to ensure that you are taking the courses you need for college acceptance. If your school employs a counselor who specializes in athletics, talk directly to that person. Otherwise, begin communicating with the counselor for your grade level. If, as in some schools, a counselor has been assigned to you for your high school years but for one reason or another is unable to meet your needs, seek the help of another counselor. This is no time to hesitate. You need a guidance counselor who is both knowledgeable about athletic scholarships and interested in your success.

Be aware that counselors often have many students to advise and therefore cannot usually dedicate extended amounts of time to any one student. But do not let that stop you from getting the attention you need. Make an appointment to talk to your counselor and be up front about your game plan. Don't wait to be called in.

Career counselors

Some high schools have career counselors who provide information about colleges, major academic areas of interest and possible career paths. Many career centers have computer programs and other resources that allow students to research individual college and universities.

Professional College Admissions Counselors/
Independent Educational Consultants

School-based counselors are often burdened with too many students and other duties to provide the services college-bound students need to choose a school. For a fee, independent counselors and consultants will help individual or small groups of students. Review their credentials and ask for references from satisfied clients. More on independent counselors and consultants is found in the Resources list, page 165.

Other Prospective Team Members

Teachers/Mentors

You need teammates

Many of you may have a teacher, an adult friend who knows you well and takes a special interest in you or an older student-athlete who has played at the college level. Any of these people might help you with advice and recommendations and be a good sounding board for your ideas.

Employers

Your boss or someone else at a job site where you have worked is another resource you can tap for a recommendation.

Clergy/Youth group leaders/Community leaders

If you have been active in your church, with an organization such as Boy or Girl Scouts, 4-H or YMCA, or as a volunteer in your community, the adults with whom you have worked can become part of your team. If you have coached youth sports, the parents of your players may be able to provide you with leads and recommendations.

Video photographer

Many college coaches want to see videotapes or DVDs of potential recruits, so it is important to have someone—parents, coaches or other supporters—film your athletic events that showcase your competitive skills. Professionals are available for this purpose, but hiring them can be costly. To save money, parents sometimes pool their resources and hire a videographer to film several players at an event. More on videotaping is found in Chapter 8, page 94.

Team substitutes

What do you do if you find that not all of the key players, such as your high school/club coach, parent and/or counselor, are available to help you? For example, you may not live with your parents, or for whatever reason, they may be unable to assist you. As on any sports team, when someone is unavailable, a substitute is brought into the game. A favorite teacher, adult friend or mentor can be an excellent substitute for your parent.

But what if your high school coach leaves and is replaced by a new coach who does not really get to know you or fails to view your talents as favorably as your old coach? Fortunately, you still have alternatives. Your high school's athletic director can write you a recommendation and test any skills necessary to fill out a college recruiter's information sheet, replacing the coach as a member of your team, or another one of your coaches can also help you. The following stories serve as examples.

Jason had an excellent baseball season in his junior year of high school. He received several letters from college coaches expressing interest in him and asking him to give a student recruiting form to his high school coach to fill out and return to the college. However, Jason and the rest of the team were unaware that their coach had decided to accept a job in another state. He moved before filling out Jason's recruiting forms, so Jason asked the athletic director to fill out the forms and provide a recommendation in place of his former baseball coach.

In another case, Barbara did not get along with the basketball coach at her local high school. So, she decided not to play for the high school team, even though she loved basketball and was good at it. She was fortunate to find a summer league in her city. That team traveled to other areas for games, and at the end of the season there was a championship tournament that college coaches attended. This gave Barbara the opportunity she needed to work with a coach who could recommend her, to play basketball in a competitive league, to increase her skills and to be seen by college coaches.

In each of these cases, substitutes worked out just as well or even better, so look around you for options when members of your team are unavailable or unwilling to support you.

Bring in a substitute

Communicate Your Goals

Now that you have identified key people as teammates, you will want to talk with them about your plans and ask for their assistance. "It is very important to have a clear goal and to verbalize that goal to people in the position to help you," says Ali D., former volleyball player, UCLA.

Some of your teammates already know about your interest in playing at the collegiate level as a result of your asking them to help you assess your athletic potential. Now is the time to let them know that you definitely want to compete at your sport in college and that you are actively seeking an athletic scholarship. It is also time to ask them directly for their support.

According to high school coach Russ Peterich, the responsibility for initiating and maintaining communication between you and the coach is yours. "Athletes need to let their coaches know they're interested in playing sports at the college level and are looking for an athletic scholarship. It's up to them [the athletes] to take the initiative, to get the ball rolling."

Communicating your goals helps get the word out about your plan, and it is also part of your marketing strategy. The more people who know about your goals, the more help you will have in reaching them.

Verbalize your goals

Get Organized

Being organized saves time!

Staying organized throughout the process is important. Setting up a filing system in the beginning for storing recruiting information will save you time and energy along the way, enabling you to find what you are looking for quickly, rather than searching through piles of papers every time you want something. Having a filing system reduces the risks of losing important, and perhaps irreplaceable, documents. You need a safe place to store awards, honors, transcripts and letters of recommendation that you collect, and also a way to organize the large amount of information you receive from colleges, like brochures, catalogs, applications, forms and other papers. We suggest you obtain or arrange to borrow the organizational supplies and equipment you will need.

Organizational Supplies and Equipment Checklist

- ❏ Calendar
- ❏ File folders
- ❏ A file box or cabinet
- ❏ A map of U.S.
- ❏ Photocopies of the College Information Worksheet for every college you are contacting (see page 160 for a blank copy of this worksheet.)
- ❏ Photocopies of the Materials Tracking Chart (see page 162 for a blank copy of this chart.)
- ❏ Postage stamps
- ❏ A postage scale or see USPS.com for a postage rate calculator
- ❏ Pens, highlighters
- ❏ A stapler
- ❏ Scissors
- ❏ Package of white bond paper
- ❏ Envelopes (letter size and 9 x 12 inch manila)
- ❏ Computer
- ❏ Printer
- ❏ Photocopier
- ❏ Fax machine

Use your calendar!

Calendar

A calendar is key! You will need it for reminding yourself of the tasks you need to do and for recording important deadlines. The best calendar for this purpose shows a month at time and has enough space to write in. Hang it on your wall, where you can see it easily, possibly near your desk or work area. Get used to looking at it daily. It won't help to have a calendar if you don't use it. (A sample calendar with a sample month filled in is shown on page 57.) You can also use an electronic calendar, if that's more convenient.

Sample Calendar for High School Student-Athlete

March 2007

SUN	MON	TUES	WED	THURS	FRI	SAT
				1 Ask Coach for recommendation	2	3 Sent initial contact letter to Big Top Col.
4	5	6	7 Received player profile sheet from State U.	8	9	10
11	12 Ask Mr. Thomas for recommendation	13	14	15 Mailed player profile sheet to State U.	16	17
18	19	20 Meet w/ guidance counselor	21 Call Coach Anderson	22	23 Sent video to Acorn U.	24
25	26	27	28	29 Sent sports resume kit to Rockwell St.	30	31

Mark deadlines in red!

File Folders

You will need file folders and file labels for saving your clippings, honors, awards, schedules, transcripts, SAT/ACT scores, letters of recommendation, etc. You will also need separate file folders for each college or university that sends you information. Be prepared! You will receive huge amounts of materials. Each time you receive a letter or brochure from a college, file it in its own folder right away. You might also want a "needs attention" file, where you will put letters that need a response or profile sheets that need to be filled out by you or your high school coach. You will want to look at this file frequently to make sure you have done what is requested of you. On your calendar mark any deadlines for returning information to colleges.

Storage for Files

If your parents have a small metal filing cabinet you can use, that's great. Otherwise, you can buy one at a used office furniture store or at a garage sale. A less expensive alternative is to buy a couple of heavy cardboard file boxes at an office supply store. These provide excellent storage for all the files you are going to fill.

Map of U.S.

This is good for helping you see where the colleges you are considering are actually located. Especially if you are looking at colleges across the country, a map can help you pinpoint locations and get you to thinking about such things as distance from home, weather and proximity to a major city.

College Information Worksheet

A great way to organize information you gather about every college and athletic program that interests you is by using the College Information Worksheet. A blank worksheet is provided for you on page 160. Photocopy this worksheet as many times as you need, one sheet for each school. As you collect information, record it in the spaces provided. Fill in the worksheets as you go along so that at the end you will have all of the information you need in one place. The worksheet will help you keep important information about individual schools at your fingertips.

Materials Tracking Chart

The Materials Tracking Chart will assist you in keeping track of when you requested certain information and when you received it. It will also help you remember important deadlines. A blank Materials Tracking Chart has been provided for you on page 162. Every time you send out or receive any correspondence, write the date in the appropriate box on the chart. Do this for each school you're interested in. This way, at any time you can glance at the chart and know exactly what has been sent or received and when.

A sample filled-in Materials Tracking Chart is shown below:

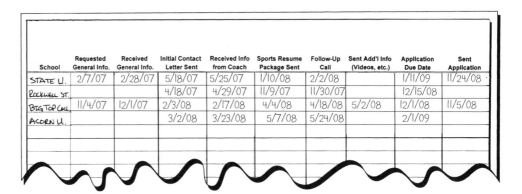

School	Requested General Info.	Received General Info.	Initial Contact Letter Sent	Received Info from Coach	Sports Resume Package Sent	Follow-Up Call	Sent Add'l Info (Videos, etc.)	Application Due Date	Sent Application
STATE U.	2/7/07	2/28/07	5/18/07	5/25/07	1/10/08	2/2/08		1/11/09	11/24/08
ROCKWELL ST.			4/18/07	4/29/07	11/9/07	11/30/07		12/15/08	
BIG TOP COLL.	11/4/07	12/1/07	2/3/08	2/17/08	4/4/08	4/18/08	5/2/08	12/1/08	11/5/08
ACORN U.			3/2/08	3/23/08	5/7/08	5/24/08		2/1/09	

Postage Supplies and Mailing Tips

Keeping postage stamps on hand will save you a trip to the post office each time you have something to mail. Another handy item is a postage scale. Fairly inexpensive, it will enable you to put the exact amount of postage on your envelope. Weighing a thick packet of materials on a postal scale will help ensure it is not returned to you for insufficient postage. This can also save you time.

A word of caution: There are times when you should mail an important piece of mail from the post office and send it with a Certificate of Mailing (available from your post office). Any mailing with a deadline attached should be mailed this way to provide you with a record of the date you mailed the item. In case the item gets lost along the way or misplaced once it gets to its destination, this is your best and most cost-effective way of proving that you mailed it before the deadline. USPS.com lists postal rates.

Other Supplies

You can store other supplies such as paper, pens, highlighters, scissors, stapler, envelopes and postage stamps in your file storage box or cabinet. Keeping them together so they will be handy is a good idea so you won't have to search all over the house when you need them quickly.

Buy a package of bond paper at an office supply store to use for correspondence. Stick with white rather than colored paper. You can buy matching white envelopes for sending letters or for mailing information coaches have requested. For your Sports Resume Kit you will need 9 x 12 inch manila envelopes. You can also buy these in packages of a dozen or more at office supply stores. Of course, the more you are able to send information online, the lower your cost for supplies and stamps.

Summary

- Putting together a game plan for success increases your chances of receiving an athletic scholarship.

- Gathering the best team to assist you in reaching your goals is as important to you as a coach's selecting an all-star team to help win a championship.

- Starting early in your high school career to put your game plan together increases your chance for success.

- Creating an organizational system for recruiting paperwork makes it easier to stay on top of deadlines, correspondence and other important recruiting information.

Now it's time to begin a systematic search for the college that best fits both your scholastic and sports needs. Chapter 7 discusses important criteria to consider as you search for the right college.

Identify the Best College for You

"You must first decide that collegiate athletics is what you want to do for four years. Pick out a college or university that offers what you want academically first, and then look into its athletic program. Remember, if you are not happy with the school, you won't be happy with the athletic program."

Renee Luers-Gillispie
Coach, women's softball
University of Central Florida

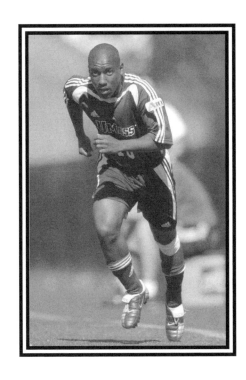

Beginning Your Search

Now that you have selected a team of people to help you win a sports scholarship and organized a system for keeping track of information and staying on top of deadlines, it's time to begin researching colleges and sending out letters of interest to college coaches. As an athlete, you will want to focus on colleges that offer good programs in both sports and scholastics.

Academics first!

You can identify such colleges by using one of two approaches. The first is to locate all schools that present scholarships in your sport, and then look at other factors—primarily the academic program—to narrow your choices. The second approach is to first select all of the schools that meet your academic requirements and then narrow your focus to schools that offer scholarships in your sport. Either approach may lead you to the same conclusion, but we recommend academic considerations first and athletics second.

Education Should Be Your Top Priority

For any college-bound student, finding the right college takes research and careful consideration. As a student-athlete you have even more to think about than academics. Your first instinct may be to go wherever you can get an athletic scholarship and play your sport, but you need to look at the entire picture when selecting a college. After all, the primary reason for going to college is to get an education, so you want to look closely at the collegiate academic environment first. Competing in sports, though a worthwhile endeavor, should be secondary.

Pro? Probably not

While you might go on to play professional sports, the fact is the athletic careers of most college athletes end with their eligibility. According to NCAA President Myles Brand, "Your likelihood of ultimate recruitment into professional leagues is small, so for almost all of you, your years as a student-athlete in college will be the peak of your athletics experience. A college degree, however, lasts a lifetime. So go for the education first."

Russell White, a former professional football player and collegiate superstar, was touted to be a first-round draft pick after his junior season with the University of California at Berkeley. White, however, decided to pass up the draft, choosing instead to stay in school, finish his senior year and graduate. White said in a 1993 article in the *Los Angeles Times*, "The best feeling of my life was...getting that diploma. You can't play football forever, you know. People can take your money, take your job, take your car, even take your wife, but that degree—that's mine. Nobody [can] take that away."

TABLE 6:
PROBABILITY OF COMPETING IN ATHLETICS
BEYOND THE HIGH SCHOOL INTERSCHOLASTIC LEVEL

Student-Athletes	Men's Basketball	Women's Basketball	Football	Baseball	Men's Ice Hockey	Men's Soccer
High School Student-Athletes	549,500	456,900	983,600	455,300	29,900	321,400
High School Senior Student-Athletes	157,000	130,500	281,000	130,100	8,500	91,800
NCAA Student-Athletes	15,700	14,400	56,500	25,700	3,700	18,200
NCAA Freshman Roster Positions	4,500	4,100	16,200	7,300	1,100	5,200
NCAA Senior Student-Athletes	3,500	3,200	12,600	5,700	800	4,100
NCAA Student-Athletes Drafted	44	32	250	600	33	76
Percent High School to NCAA	2.9	3.1	5.8	5.6	12.9	5.7
Percent NCAA to Professional	1.3	1.0	2.0	10.5	4.1	1.9
Percent High School to Professional	0.03	0.02	0.09	0.5	0.4	0.08

NCAA 2006

The Initial Contact Letter

Start the recruiting process yourself!

Once you narrow your list of schools, as the rest of this chapter instructs, you will want to prepare and send *initial contact letters*. These can be sent by e-mail or through the postal service. One letter should be sent to the college coach at each school you're interested in, introducing yourself and your interest in the sports program and requesting more information. (An example is shown on page 64.) This letter, which should be brief, serves the following purposes:

- Starts the recruiting process by bringing YOU to the attention of the coach
- Causes the coach to start a file for you in his or her office to keep track of your athletic talents and your progress
- Results in the coach sending back the information you requested so that you can better evaluate the college and its athletic program

You can expect to receive the requested information within two weeks, or longer if that sport is in its season. Additionally, expect the coach to send along a *player profile sheet* or direct you to fill one out on the institution's website. A standard form that many college coaches use to get information about an interested student-athlete, the player profile sheet usually includes questions regarding background information as well as academic and athletic history. The college coach keeps it on file and updates it periodically as new information becomes available. A sample player profile sheet can be seen on pages 66 and 67.

MARK ENGLISH
1213 Waterford Drive
Petaluma, California 94952
(707) 555-9448
e-mail: mark@soccercleat.com

June 1, 20xx

Mr. Sam Tighner
Head Coach, Men's Soccer
Department of Athletics
Whitney College
3498 University Parkway
Lambert, Illinois 78900

Dear Coach Tighner:

I am writing to express my interest in the men's soccer program at Whitney College. Next fall I will be a junior at Laguna High School in Petaluma, California, and am beginning to look at prospective colleges. I would appreciate any information that you can send me regarding your program, school and the availability of athletic scholarships.

Thank you very much.

Sincerely,

Mark English

When to Send the Initial Contact Letter

Our survey of college coaches reveals that most of them want to be contacted by students who are beginning their junior year of high school or even earlier. We suggest sending the initial contact letter in your sophomore year. Here is what a few of the coaches say about timing the initial contact letter:

"Contact coaches early on in your high school career—such as during your sophomore year—and then keep them updated."
Randy Thomas, director, cross-country/track and field, Boston College, Massachusetts

"Contact college coaches during summer prior to junior year in high school in a written letter."
Beth Anders, coach, field hockey, Old Dominion University, Virginia

"Contact coaches early, either in the sophomore year or the beginning of the junior year."
Kim Sutton, coach, women's soccer, CSU Chico, California

MEN'S SPORTS

Baseball	Soccer
Basketball	Tennis
Cross Country	Track & Field
Football	Volleyball
Golf	Water Polo
	Wrestling

WOMEN'S SPORTS

Basketball	Softball
Cross Country	Swimming & Diving
Golf	Tennis
Gymnastics	Track & Field
Rowing	Vollybal
Soccer	Water Polo

YOUR SPORT _____

STATE U. PROSPECTIVE STUDENT-ATHLETE INFORMATION SHEET

Today's Date: _____ Your Birthdate: _____ S.S. #: _____

Full Name: _____ Phone: ( ) _____ Cell: ( ) _____

Nickname/Preferred First Name: _____ Religion (optional): _____

Address: _____
      Street   City   State   Zip

E-mail Address: _____

Father's Name: _____ Occupation: _____

Address: _____
      Street   City   State   Zip

Phone: ( ) _____ Cell: ( ) _____ E-mail Address: _____

Mother's Name: _____ Occupation: _____

Address: _____
      Street   City   State   Zip

Phone: ( ) _____ Cell: ( ) _____ E-mail Address: _____

College Parent(s) Attended: _____ # Brothers _____ # Sisters _____

State U. Student/Friends /Alumni you know: _____

Year in School: _____ H.S. Graduation Date: _____ Place of Birth: _____

ATHLETIC PARTICIPATION

Height: _____ Weight: _____ Uniform Playing Number/School Colors: _____

H.S. Playing Position/Events: _____ L or R Handed: _____

H.S./Club Statistics (Please list best times/marks/scores): _____

_____

_____

Second Sport You Play: _____ Does your H.S./Club videotape events? _____

H.S. Coach: _____

Coach's Home Phone: ( ) _____ School Phone: ( ) _____ Cell: ( ) _____

Club Team: _____ Coach: _____ Home Phone: ( ) _____ Cell: ( ) _____

ACADEMICS

High School: _____   High School Principal: _____   School Phone: (   ) _____

High School Counselor: _____   Phone: (   ) _____

High School Address: _____

         Street   City   State   Zip

High School Website: _____

Your GPA: _____   Class Rank: _____   SAT Verbal/Math: _____   ACT Score: _____   Favorite Class: _____

Academic Study Interests/Possible College Major: _____

Academic Honors: _____

_____

Colleges you are considering (in order):   1. _____   2. _____

3. _____   4. _____   5. _____

STATE U. ATHLETIC INFORMATION QUESTIONS

1. What camps, tournaments or events will you participate in this summer? Please list where and when.

   1. _____

   2. _____

   3. _____

   4. _____

   5. _____

   6. _____

2. Is it OK for STATE U. to make direct phone or e-mail contact with you? If yes, please specify the best day(s) of the week and time to call.

_____

3. Why are you considering STATE U.?

_____

4. Have you visited STATE U. before? _____   If yes, when? _____

5. If you have not taken the SAT/ACT test, when will you take it? _____

6. What are your sport/career ambitions? _____

Please sign your name if it is OK for STATE U. to access your high school transcript/academic record for admission purposes.

Signature: _____

Where to Send the Initial Contact Letter

College guides

Gather data on colleges

Before you can send the initial contact letter, you need to gather general information about colleges so that you can decide which ones you want to know more about. Luckily for you, the bookshelves in counseling centers as well as in public libraries are filled with directories and guides to help you choose a college. Bookstores and online booksellers also carry these guides, so if you do not have access to a counseling center or library, you may want to buy one or two to use at home. If so, make sure they were recently published. Several of the most complete print guides are listed in the Resources list on page 163.

Website directories make it easy to look at colleges on your home or school computer. Some of these are free; others are fee-based. (A few of the best sites are listed on page 165.) Most universities have websites that virtually walk you around their campus and give you up-to-date information about their school.

Academic guides: Look through college academic guides and college websites and pick a maximum of 30 schools that interest you. You will want to look at various factors as they pertain to each school. But your primary goal at this point is to identify those schools that broadly meet your requirements so that you can later assess each school and then narrow your choices. Some of the factors you may use to access schools are introduced later in this chapter.

Athletic guides: After you select a broad group of schools that appear to meet your general academic considerations, you will want to determine the following:

Check the level of competition

- Do they offer your sport?
- What is the level of athletic competition (Division I, II or III)?
- Do they award scholarships in your sport?

Several directories that focus on collegiate athletics can provide this information. One is *Peterson's Sports Scholarships and College Athletic Programs*, an excellent resource for locating the colleges that offer your sport, as well as for the contact information (name, address, e-mail address, phone number) of the colleges and coaches.

Look up the 30 or fewer schools that you selected to see what kind of programs they present. If they play your sport and have scholarships to award, you will want to send the initial contact letter to each coach as described above.

Other Ways to Get Information

To learn about specific colleges, you can write or call the admissions office to request general information. (See sample letter on page 70.) If a coach sends you only his or her athletic program brochure, ask the admissions office to send you brochures, catalogs and other literature about the college. Your high school counseling office or career center and your public library may even have some of this material on hand, especially if the colleges that interest you are located in your state. Otherwise, go to the college's website to request more information.

Talking to people who are familiar with a specific college, such as alumni or current students, can give you excellent first-hand information from people who have blazed the trail before you. Visiting the colleges can also provide you with valuable information. On the visit you can get a feel for the school by asking questions of students and faculty. Be sure to take time to walk around the campus and soak in the atmosphere. This can give you a pretty good idea about how you would fit in at a particular college.

When you receive all the information you requested, you will be able to narrow your list to those schools that meet your specific academic and athletic criteria. After looking at the information sent to you by each school and coach and determining which institutions generally match your needs, you can begin to aggressively pursue an athletic scholarship.

MARK ENGLISH
1213 Waterford Drive
Petaluma, California 94952
(707) 555-9448
e-mail: mark@soccercleat.com

June 1, 20xx

Director
Office of Admissions
Whitney College
3498 University Parkway
Lambert, Illinois 78900

Dear Director:

I am interested in knowing more about Whitney College. I will be a junior next year
and am beginning to look at colleges. Please send me general, admissions and financial
aid information about your school. Thank you.

Sincerely,

Mark English

What to Consider When Choosing a College

There is no one perfect college. David D. Cuttino, former dean of undergraduate admissions, Tufts University, Massachusetts, advises high school students to be realistic: "Recognize that there is no such thing as Utopia University. All have their strengths and weaknesses, which vary from student to student. Finding 'the best college' should be based on your own personal choice and not an arbitrary rating system. Do your own thinking and analysis. The best college should be one that is best for you."

Some factors that will help in your search are listed in Table 7 below, and are explained in detail later in this chapter. Some of these factors may be more important to you than others. Read through and then develop your own list of criteria to use when looking at colleges.

While you will want to consider all aspects of the college experience when researching your choices, you should look first at nonathletic considerations and then identify what's important to you as an athlete.

What are your major interests?

TABLE 7:
FACTORS TO CONSIDER IN CHOOSING A COLLEGE

Nonathletic Factors	Athletic Factors

Location of college
    proximity to home
    climate, geography and demographics
	Availability of sports scholarships
	
	Level of competition

Campus environment
    size of institution
    housing options
    extracurricular activities
	Time commitment, length of season
	
	Athletic department attitude

Nature of student body	Coaching
	      staff
	      style

Academic environment
    admission requirements
    quality and quantity of courses and degree requirements
    availability of your major area(s) of interest
    student/teacher ratio
    quality of faculty
	Importance of academics to athletic department
	
	Facilities
	
	Services

Cost
    availability of financial aid/scholarships
    employment opportunities
	Budget for your sport
	
	Teammates

Graduation rate of athletes in your sport	Reputation of team

Nonathletic Factors

Location

A school's location may be of major importance to you and your family. Some high school counselors advise that you think about distance from home before any other factors. Considerations may include:

- ease and expense of traveling to and from college
- cost of calling home (to family and/or friends), unless you have a free long-distance cell phone plan
- emotional considerations/homesickness
- climate
- environment — areas differ from one another in cultural aspects, social mores, etc.
- geography — on the coast, in the mountains or plains
- demographics — large metropolitan area vs. suburban or rural campus

Check a map

One way to help visualize the impact of location is to sit down with your parents and study a map of the United States. Looking at the map, decide how far away from home (in miles) you are willing to travel to school. Using that distance as your radius, draw a big red circle, with your hometown at the center of the circle. Inside your circle is the area you want to target when looking for a school. Too inflexible? Maybe, but location can be very important.

Campus environment

Some factors to consider include:

- size of the institution
- campus setting
- cultural opportunities
- housing
- extracurricular and recreational activities

Size of institution: The size of the campus and the number of students can have a dramatic impact on your college experience. For example, Michigan State University, a large public institution, has over 35,000 students. Compare that with the less than 4,000 student population at University of the Pacific, a private college in Stockton, California, set in an agricultural valley. The environments on these two campuses differ strikingly, so it is important for you to determine the atmosphere in which you would feel most comfortable and perform at your best, both academically and athletically.

At colleges with a smaller population, where class sizes are smaller and there is perhaps less competition, students may feel a part of campus life sooner. Larger campuses, on the other hand, can be more exciting because there is opportunity to meet and be challenged by many different people and enjoy a variety of cultural and educational opportunities. Small-college supporters say they like being big fish in a small pond, while advocates of larger institutions point to the stimulation and range of opportunities offered in a broader, more diverse environment.

Housing options: Evaluating housing facilities is important in considering prospective schools. Is there enough campus housing available for all students who want it, or is scrambling for housing each year going to be a major problem? Private dorms, cooperatives and other living groups have alternative housing opportunities. Fraternities and sororities are popular on some campuses and often provide housing.

You will want to investigate the availability and variety of housing options on campuses that interest you. If on-campus housing is not available, be sure to research the availability and cost of housing in the surrounding community.

Extracurricular and recreational activities:
If extracurricular recreational opportunities are important to you, check out what's happening on or near the campuses under your consideration.

- Are extracurricular activities available, such as student political organizations, intramural sports or musical theater?
- Are you into rock climbing, scuba diving, hiking or horseback riding?
- Do you yearn to get out into the quiet countryside, or is exploring the excitement of city life your favorite way to spend leisure time?
- Will you need your own car or is there adequate public transportation?

Nature of student body:
The makeup of the student body can influence your collegiate experience. Some questions you may want to ask are:

- Is the school co-ed or all women/all men?
- Do most students live on or near campus or do they commute?
- Where do the students generally come from?
- Is the school culturally and ethnically diversified?
- Is it public or private?
- Is it a religion-based school?
- What attracts most students to this school?

Academic environment

The academic climate of colleges and universities can vary widely. Significant areas for you to research are:

- Admission and graduation requirements
- Demands of the curriculum
- Quality of the courses in your major areas of interest
- Accessibility of the classes you need

Admission requirements and difficulty of courses:
Many schools have achieved nationwide reputations for their academic standards. While some institutions are renowned for their selectivity in the admissions process, others are known for maintaining their rigorous standards once you have been accepted. You might want to consider the competitive level of admission requirements and the difficulty of the classes. Think about whether you would be more successful in a highly competitive or a more nurturing academic atmosphere.

Availability of your major area(s) of interest:
Although you may not be ready to choose your major at this point, you are probably aware of the academic areas in which you're most interested, for example, history, English, math, biology. Find out whether the colleges you are considering offer courses in these areas. Not only is it

Where do you fit in?

important for your future to investigate the school's curriculum, but as a student-athlete, your knowledge of these areas may keep you under a college coach's consideration.

Finding out in what academic subjects the college is strong and whether your major areas of interest are open or impacted is important. Ask about the size of the classes and about the teacher/student ratio. Also, research how long it takes the average student in your major areas of interest to earn a degree.

*Can you graduate
in 4 years?*

Tufts University's David D. Cuttino, longtime dean of undergraduate admissions, advises high school seniors: "You are preparing for a future you cannot anticipate and for careers that have yet to be created. What will your college choices be if, and when, you change you mind?"

Chris Porch, former Division I soccer player, concurs: "If you have an idea of what you want to do after college, find out how the curriculum fits those plans. But I'd advise recruits to check out the breadth of the curriculum as well, because you will probably change your mind."

Cost

For each college you are considering, research the cost of tuition, room and board, books and supplies and other expenses, and don't forget to factor in travel costs. For example, if the college you select is in New York state and your family lives in Oregon, figure your travel expenses for crossing the U.S. at least a couple of times a year. Greater distances may also mean higher telephone bills for calling home, although some cell phone users have unlimited long-distance plans. Also consider any purchases you will have to make, for example, a bike, car or new clothing for warmer or colder climates.

Cost varies

Another cost factor that can have a huge impact on expenses is out-of-state tuition. Higher fees, often amounting to several thousand dollars a year, are charged to non-residents at *public institutions*. Sometimes out-of-state tuition is waived for recruited athletes, but make sure you check this out. More information on financial aid is found in Chapter 12.

Although you need to find out whether scholarships are awarded in your sport and whether financial aid is available, don't place undue emphasis in the early stages of discovery on cost and let it sway you from pursuing the college of your choice. Often, colleges that charge more have more financial assistance available. So, consider cost just one of the factors in selecting an institution. If you think you may need to work while attending school, another area you should explore is the availability of jobs on campus or nearby. Information about work-study programs is found in Chapter 12, pages 135 and 136.

Graduation rate of athletes

What is the *graduation rate* among athletes in general at the schools you are considering? What is the graduation rate among athletes in your sport? How long does it generally take athletes in your sport to graduate? The answers to these questions are very important. While the relatively high number of college athletes who fail to graduate has dropped in the past few years and the push to graduate athletes continues to increase, some institutions have a stronger commitment than others to academics and graduating their athletes. The NCAA keeps yearly statistics on the graduation rate of member institutions. You can request this information from NCAA or ask the institutions themselves. The NAIA provides this information, too. See the Resources list on page 164 for these associations' contact information.

Athletic Factors

After looking at the academic aspects of an institution, you should then consider its athletic program and what it has to offer you. Consider the following factors when evaluating a school's athletic program and how appropriate it is for you.

Availability of scholarships

After locating a printed or online reference guide to college sports, see which of the colleges you have identified as attractive to you academically also give sports scholarships. Or contact coaches at schools that interest you to find out whether scholarships are available.

Level of competition

Because there are many levels of competition in collegiate athletic programs, determining whether the schools you are considering match your skill level is important. Your high school or club coach can perhaps help you with this. Finding out to which division a school belongs provides a general guideline for judging the competitiveness of its athletic program. For instance, a Division II school's baseball program is probably less competitive than a Division I baseball program. However, this distinction between divisions does not always hold true.

According to Joan Powell, NCAA and United States Volleyball Association (USAV) national referee and former volleyball coach at Coronado High School, Colorado, "There are Division II teams that are more competitive than Division I." Find out more about athletic divisions in Chapter 3.

Be realistic!

Using the information you gathered in the process of assessing your athletic abilities and potential, think about whether you can actually play for a particular school and whether the level of competition is appropriate for your skill level. For example, if you found in your assessment that you probably are not going to be a Division I prospect, do not expect a full-ride scholarship from a Division I school. Be realistic.

Another consideration when selecting an appropriate athletic program is your potential playing time. Even if you feel you can compete at the level of a particular team, what are your chances of starting or playing consistently?

"Don't be afraid to ask the coach where he or she thinks you'll fit on the team. Ask whether you'll be an impact player or will it be a year or two before you'll be able to play," advises Kim Sutton, women's soccer coach, CSU Chico, California.

Consider these questions when looking for programs that match your skill level:

- Do you want to play for a program only if you can be a star, or will you be happy to accept limited playing time?
- Do you want to step into a program and play right away, or are you willing to wait a few years before getting your chance?

Being on athletic scholarship requires that you fulfill certain obligations to have your scholarship renewed each year. Even if you sit on the bench your entire collegiate athletic career, you have to practice, work out and follow the same rigorous regimen and regulations that a starter does. Although all team members are important regardless of their roles, a less competitive program might afford you more of a chance to actually participate come game time.

Player or benchwarmer?

Patrick Atwell, baseball coach, Quincy University, Illinois, states, "Student-athletes, coaches and parents have to be realistic in picking a level in which the student-athlete can participate. It is better for the player to go to a school where he or she can play than a school where he or she will ride the bench."

Time commitment, length of season

Attempt to determine what would be expected of you as a student-athlete at the schools you are considering. Here are some examples of questions to ask:

- How many months of the year is an athlete expected to practice and participate in your sport?
- What is the length of your sport's season?
- How many hours a day do athletes in your sport practice/workout during the season? In the off-season?
- Does participation in your sport require athletes to begin practicing before school starts?
- Are athletes required to practice or play during school breaks and vacations?

These are important questions to ask when you are considering schools and their athletic programs. Generally, the more competitive the program, the greater the expected time commitment, although there are limitations on the amount of practice time, as set by athletic association rules.

Tough academic competition for athletes

"The college athlete is expected to compete in the classroom against other students who were studying while the student-athlete was expending great energy and time in 20-hour-a-week practices," says Stan Morrison, athletic director, University of California, Irvine.

Athletic department's attitude

How does the athletic department treat its athletes? How much support does your sport receive from the athletic department? For answers to these questions, student-athletes who are already in the program can be reliable sources of information. If you know an athlete in your sport at a school that interests you, contact the person and ask how he or she feels about the athletic program. Other questions to ask:

- Is your sport considered minor or major at the school?
- Does the athletic department promote the sport?

When you visit the campus, seek out the company of other athletes and ask these questions. This is no time to hold back. Dominic S., former UCLA football player, advises, "Talk to your potential future teammates. Observe their attitudes and their level of happiness in the program."

Coaching

Ask athletes to rate coaches

Staff: In larger programs, you may have less contact with the head coach than with the assistants during your first couple of years, so it is important to try to communicate and feel comfortable with as many coaches as possible during the recruiting period. For example, if you are an offensive lineman, you may want to talk with the coach responsible for your position in addition to the head coach. Ask how long the coaches have been with the program. If there seem to have been frequent changes in the coaching staff, ask why. Ask about their backgrounds: Where have they coached before? If you visit the school, ask other athletes in your sport what they think of the coaching. This can give you significant information.

Mike P., former football player, Harvard University, advises high school student-athletes to "look at the coaches' commitment to the athletic program and pay particular attention to the attitudes of players toward their coaches."

"You must get along with coaches, as well as teammates. These are the people you will spend the majority of your time with," says former Division I collegiate water polo player Chuck M.

"Talk to other players in your sport and find out how they feel about the coaching staff. They will tell you things you can't possibly find out by just talking to a coach who's trying to recruit you," says a Division II men's lacrosse player.

Style: An important factor to consider is how your particular skills fit in with a coach's style. For example, if you are a running back, you may want to look at football programs that feature a running attack. Or, if you play a finesse style of soccer, you probably won't want to be part of a kick-and-run offense. A good way to determine coaching style is to personally attend a contest involving the schools you are considering, if possible. Another way is to ask the coach or players on the team.

Importance of academics to athletic department

To excel in sports as well as the classroom is extremely challenging. The athletic department and its coaches, under pressure to create winning teams, can sometimes lose sight of what the student-athlete is really in college for: to get an education and to graduate. It is especially difficult if the athletic department's sole interest in you is as an athlete, not as a student.

"The athletic department did not emphasize getting top grades. They pushed the athletes to maintain a 'C' average to keep their eligibility. I think that was wrong," says a former Division I volleyball player.

Arizona State University Director of Athletics Lisa Love says, "The model at Arizona State University is to compete at the highest level of intercollegiate competition while graduating our Sun Devil student-athletes. ASU athletics serves to further the mission of the university and we actively seek talented recruits who set their sites on excelling both athletically and academically. We are committed to that success which best defines amateur sports in a university environment."

Understanding the academic philosophies of the athletic departments of schools you are considering is crucial. Here are questions you may want to ask:

• Are academic tutors and counselors available for student-athletes?

- Are student-athletes encouraged to do well in school?
- What is the graduation rate of student-athletes in your sport?

Talk to coaches at colleges that interest you and check with current student-athletes about the department's attitude toward academics.

Facilities

Find out what athletic facilities are available for each school and whether they are utilized by your sport. Tim M., former soccer player at CSU Fresno, California, advises interested student-athletes to "...take note of the athletic facilities and how they suit your needs. For example, if you need to play with your ankles taped every day, make sure the training facility can accommodate this."

Other factors to investigate:

- Is a weight room available?
- What surface does the team compete upon, for example, grass or all-weather field or track?
- How convenient is it to get to the athletic facilities?
- How far away are the locker rooms from where you must practice and work out?

Other athletes

One of the most important sources for information about college athletics in general and athletic programs in particular is former or current student-athletes. Of those we interviewed, all were in agreement about the value of student-athletes talking to their potential team members while researching colleges and their athletic programs. Here's what a few of them had to say:

Ask questions of players

"The greatest input one can get about the school and the athletic program is from the student-athletes themselves. It's extremely important to ask as many questions as possible that pertain to life as a college athlete and life as an athlete at that particular school. In other words, find out what are the expectations and responsibilities at that college and compare them with responses from athletes at other schools. As a rule, the more information you gather, the more informed your decision will become, and ultimately, it will lead to a more successful one."

Bob B., former volleyball player, UC San Diego

"I would definitely spend the majority of my time with the members of the team, not the coach or the administration. You'll get your most important questions answered honestly by your potential future teammates. Remember, coaches are on their best behavior while recruiting—it's important to get the 'inside scoop' from the people they coach."

Jennifer P., former soccer player, Stanford University

"Make it a point to observe how the athletes from the team interact with the rest of the student body. A great part of the college experience, even for the student-athlete, is based on diversity and the ability to interact with others who have divergent interests."

Kurt Z., former tennis player, University of Pennsylvania

An Alternative to Four-Year Institutions: Community Colleges

4-year colleges not for everyone

So far this chapter has been about the selection process for four-year colleges. But what about student-athletes who are not bound for four-year colleges or are not attending a four-year program right after high school? One of the best alternatives for the student-athlete to consider is a community college.

Community colleges (called *junior colleges* in some areas) are two-year educational institutions. They are an excellent alternative to the four-year college, allowing students two years to grow physically as well as socially, and to improve their level of academic and athletic performance in a cost-effective manner before continuing on for a four-year degree. Community colleges may be the answer for students who do not qualify for four-year colleges because of insufficient course work, grades below acceptable levels or non-qualifying entrance test scores.

Jill McCormick, women's swim and water polo coach at Santa Rosa Junior College in northern California, believes there are many benefits to attending a good community college for the first two years of higher education. To help student athletes decide between a community college or four-year institution, she developed the following list of questions for student-athletes to ask themselves:

- Am I socially secure? Am I mature enough to go away from home, live and study on my own, make new friends, etc?
- Are my/my family's finances sufficient to pay my college expenses? If not, is there enough other financial assistance available?
- Am I academically prepared? Can I compete scholastically at the four-year college level?
- Do I know what I want to major in? If not, have I at least identified my strong areas of interest?
- Can I compete in my sport at the four-year level, based on my physical maturation, level of competition and skill level?

Is community college right for you?

"If the student can answer 'yes' to all those questions, I advise them to go right into a four-year college," says McCormick. But if, after soul searching and considering the input of parents, coaches and high school teachers and counselors, the student answers "no" to any of these questions, McCormick believes a community college can offer as good a general education—and in some cases, a better one—than a four-year institution.

Environment and cost considerations

Community colleges are often smaller than four-year schools and offer extra support services. Their more intimate environment can feel more comfortable to students, helping them to mature socially.

According to the College Board's publication, *Trends in College Pricing, 2006*, "For students who cannot or who chose not to pay the higher costs of four-year schools, community colleges are a real bargain. Tuition and fees average about $2,272 a year. The average comparable tuition and fees at a public four-year college or university is $5,836 a year. Compared with the tuition at private schools, the difference is much greater."

Academic opportunities

Students can improve their academic skills and build a respectable grade point average at community colleges while getting general education classes out of the way. Community colleges typically admit students regardless of their previous academic history and offer remediation classes to develop college-level math and English skills.

Athletic opportunities

Besides presenting the chance to improve your academic record in preparation for transferring to a four-year college, many community colleges have outstanding athletic programs. Such programs offer skill-building and playing time opportunities not always found at the four-year college level. Many athletes are recruited by college coaches from the ranks of community college sports. What's more, some community colleges award athletic scholarships. To find these, consult an athletic director or coach at the community college that interests you, or contact the National Junior College Athletic Association (NJCAA). See the Resources list on page 164.

A Division II Midwestern community college coach who responded to our survey believes that most baseball players get more playing time at the community college level than they do on a four-year college team during their freshman and sophomore years. Furthermore, these players can often get the individual coaching that enables them to improve their skills. This coach firmly believes that "many of the players who aren't mature enough to play college ball out of high school improve their skills and gain needed experience playing community college ball. Then after two years, or sometimes even one, they're recruited by four-year college teams, and some are awarded scholarships."

Early chance to contribute at a 2-year school

Because a number of community colleges are "feeder" schools for four-year programs, high school recruits are often advised by four-year coaches to apply to certain community colleges. They know that these athletes will be given more one-on-one coaching as freshmen and sophomores and will get the chance to grow and mature, making it possible for them to compete later at the four-year level. In other cases, coaches might wish an athlete could come directly into their athletic program but they know that he or she lacks the academics for college admission and therefore needs the remediation courses available at a community college.

"Particularly in baseball and basketball, two years in a good community college program provides excellent training for the more competitive college sports," says California high school golf coach Russ Peterich. In addition to experiencing a higher level of play than the athlete experienced in high school, community college programs usually have summer programs and provide year-round training.

"Oftentimes, athletes who would ride the bench for the first two years at a four-year institution will get a lot of much-needed playing time if they go to a community college first. This invaluable experience and skill-building can lead to a scholarship, whereas the same athlete wouldn't get the nod from a four-year school right out of high school," explains Peterich.

Another alternative is for a graduating high school senior to consider taking a post-graduate year at a private prep school rather than going straight to a four-year college. "For some kids, it's a good option," says Sam Koch, men's soccer coach,

University of Massachusetts. "Prep schools give them an extra year to mature, both physically and academically, before going to college."

Summary

- The primary reason for going to college is to get an education.

- Only a small percentage of collegiate athletes go on to play professional sports; therefore, student-athletes need to consider many factors in addition to sports when selecting a college.

- It is up to you to determine what criteria for selecting a college are important.

- Community colleges are an excellent alternative to four-year institutions to help student-athletes develop scholastically, socially and athletically.

So far, you have requested information from a broad range of colleges and their athletic programs and narrowed down your list. The coaches have seen your name through the initial contact letter and know about your interest. Now it is time to aggressively market yourself to the schools in which you have the most interest. Chapter 8 gives step-by-step instructions on how to assemble a marketing package with the Sports Resume Kit as your chief marketing tool.

8

Build Your Sports Resume Kit

"Send resume early. Have an up-to-date videotape or DVD prepared demonstrating your athletic abilities."

Murray Rudisill
Coach, men's golf
Old Dominion University, Virginia

What is the Sports Resume Kit?

After you have compiled a list of schools that interest you overall and cross-matched them with those that fit your athletic skill level and offer scholarships in your sport, you need to sell yourself and your abilities to each of the college coaches.

You should have already asked for and received plenty of material about the general group of colleges you contacted with your initial information request letter. You may also have received questionnaires or player profile sheets that you were asked to fill out online or return by mail.

Any time a coach requests information, respond as quickly as possible. Coaches we surveyed said that many student-athletes fail to return player profile sheets in a timely manner, which can be interpreted as showing a lack of responsibility or indifference toward their schools. Unfortunately, as a result, a coach might lose interest and look to someone else who displays more enthusiasm.

Market your talents to college coaches

When To Send Your Sports Resume Kit

Since the recruiting process is ongoing, the steps we suggest can be done at various times. The same is true of compiling and sending the Sports Resume Kit. While there is no "right" time, the beginning of your junior year is probably best because it allows plenty of time to bring yourself to a coach's attention and for the recruiting process to take place. Sending it at this time also allows you two more school years to grow and add to your accomplishments. During this time you can update coaches with new information. If you send the Sports Resume Kit much earlier, you probably will not have accumulated enough athletic and academic data to highlight your abilities. However, if you have sufficient data at a younger age, send it earlier. If you are beginning the process later, then certainly you should compile and send your Sports Resume Kit as soon as possible.

What Does Your Sports Resume Kit Include?

Your Sports Resume Kit includes everything the coach needs to judge whether to pursue you as a recruit and puts the information in a neat, concise package for easy reading. This is your sales kit, your attention-grabber, and in it you will showcase your talents and accomplishments so that the coach takes notice. Here is what many collegiate coaches and athletic directors say they want to see:

Sports Resume Kit: your sales package

- Cover letter
- Sports resume (a concise list of your academic, athletic and personal accomplishments)
- Letters of recommendation
- An offer to provide a sports video (part of cover letter)
- Upcoming game/sporting event schedule
- Copies of newspaper clippings and awards
- Picture of yourself (either a reprint of a good quality photo or a color photocopy)

Cover Letter

A cover letter is a one-page document that introduces your Sports Resume Kit. (A sample cover letter is shown on page 86.) The purpose of your cover letter is to:

- introduce or reintroduce yourself (whichever applies in your situation)
- acknowledge that you received the materials you requested
- confirm your interest in the college and its athletic program
- mention a mutual friend, alumnus or other person whom you and the coach have in common (if applicable)
- briefly describe the materials you have enclosed
- indicate your willingness to send a videotape and additional information upon the coach's request
- thank the coach for his or her interest

No 'Dear Coach' letters

Don't send a form letter. Margo Jonker, softball coach at Central Michigan University advises, "Write a personal letter of interest after determining the coach's name. No 'Dear Coach' letters."

You should already know the coach's name and contact information, but if not, check the college website and/or call the university's athletic department to find out the coach's name and verify the correct spelling. You can get the e-mail and mailing address and direct phone number at the same time.

Your correspondence with coaches should be neat and concise, whether you use e-mail or regular mail. If regular mail, typed correspondence is best, though a handwritten letter is fine, as long as your writing is easy to read. Make sure you proofread all correspondence before sending it out. After you have read over your letter and made corrections, it is best to let someone else review it to check for errors you might have missed. If your computer has a spell checker, be sure to use it!

Appearance counts!

Coaches say that they throw some letters from prospective recruits directly into the trash or press the delete key. Why? Because the letters are unreadable due to illegible handwriting or poor language skills, leading the coach to conclude that the student is not college material. Colleges are, after all, institutions of higher education. A carelessly written or illegible letter can quickly lead a coach to dismiss you as a serious prospect. Your correspondence should demonstrate your ability to compete in the academic world as well as showcase your athletic potential.

"The student-athlete's e-mail should be in letter format…a lot of coaches are not going to respond to 'hey coach' or 'dude.' Show me you know how to conduct yourself," says Sam Koch, men's soccer coach, University of Massachusetts.

MARK ENGLISH
1213 Waterford Drive
Petaluma, California 94952
(707) 555-9448
e-mail: mark@soccercleat.com

February 18, 20xx

Mr. Sam Tighner
Head Coach, Men's Soccer
Department of Athletics
Whitney College
3498 University Parkway
Lambert, Illinois 78900

Dear Mr. Tighner:

I am a junior midfielder at Laguna High School in Petaluma, California. As you may remember, I wrote to you some time ago to request information about your soccer program and the availability of athletic scholarships, as well as general information about Whitney College. After reading through the material you sent and filling out the player profile sheet as you requested, I am very interested in Whitney College and the possibility of playing in your soccer program.

I have enclosed my sports resume as well as other information to give you a complete picture of my academic and athletic history to date. Please note on the game schedule that I will be playing in your area next summer. I hope you will have a chance to come and see me play. In addition, I can compile a videotape at your request. Please let me know what you would like to see and I will be happy to send it to you.

Thank you for your consideration. I am excited about the soccer program at Whitney College and look forward to talking to you. I will contact you in a week or so to confirm that you received my information.

Sincerely,

Mark English

The Sports Resume

Your Sports Resume should be brief

A resume is a short summary of a person's career and qualifications typically prepared by the job applicant. It usually highlights one's accomplishments and experience and presents them in a logical format so that the reader can view at a glance all of the relevant information about a person.

A sports resume is very similar to a job resume, but instead of highlighting information necessary for gaining employment, the focus is on information necessary for gaining a place with a collegiate athletic program and ultimately winning a sports scholarship. (An example of a sports resume is provided on pages 88 and 89. The Sports Resume Worksheet on page 159 will help you organize all your information.) Your sports resume should be brief, no more than two pages, and should include the following elements:

Academic information
- Grade point average/class standing
- SAT/ACT scores
- Subject test scores
- Awards, honors

Athletic information
- Statistics
- Physical dimensions
- Tournament competition
- High-performance level teams
- Sports camps attended
- Jersey number
- Awards, honors

Personal background
- Leadership roles (class officer, president of club, etc.)
- Memberships (organizations in or out of school)
- Community involvement
- Employment
- List of references with names, addresses, telephone numbers, e-mail addresses

MARK ENGLISH
1213 Waterford Drive
Petaluma, California 94952
(707) 555-9448
E-mail: mark@soccercleat.com

Athletic

Sport:	Soccer
Position:	Midfield
Laguna High School Jersey:	#12
Sonoma Soccer Club Jersey:	#4
40-Yard Time:	4.6

Academic

GPA:	3.40
SAT Score:	1090
Anticipated Date of Graduation:	June, 2007
High School:	Laguna High School
	Petaluma, California

Personal Data

Date of Birth:	March 23, 1989
Height:	5'10"
Weight:	160 lbs.

Sports Background

2005/06 (Junior Year)
- Team 1st place, North Bay League (LHS)
- Team 1st place, Tournament of Champions (LHS)
- Team 2nd place, Club Winter League
  (Sonoma Soccer Club)

2004/05 (Sophomore Year)
- Team 1st place, North Bay League (LHS)
- Team 1st place, Viking Invitational (LHS)
- Team 2nd place, Hawaiian Rainbow International
  Youth Soccer Classic (Sonoma Soccer Club)
- Team 2nd place, CYSA State Cup
  (Sonoma Soccer Club)

Mark English
Page 2

Awards/Honors

Athletic
- Team Captain, Laguna High School (Fall 2005)
- Member, All-North Bay League Team (Fall 2004, 2005)
- Member, All-Tournament Team, Tournament of Champions (Fall 2005)
- Varsity Block Recipient (2004-05 and 2005-06)
- Member, CYSA District 5 Select Team (2005-06)

Academic
- Junior Class Representative (2005-06)
- 1st place, Optimist Club Speech Contest (2004-05)
- President, Rotary Youth Club (2004-05)
- Honor Roll (2004-05 and 2005-06)

Other Information

Other Sports
- Baseball: Pitcher/Outfielder
- Football: Place-kicker

Camps
- Liberty State University Soccer Camp (Summer 2002, 2003)

Employment
- Coach, Redwood Empire Soccer Camp (Summer 2004, 2005, 2006)

Community Service
- Junior Volunteer, Rincon Volunteer Fire Department
- Assistant Coach, Petaluma Hills Little League

References
- Mr. Daniel Anderson
  Varsity Soccer Coach, Laguna High School
  1501 Herringbone Drive, Petaluma, CA 94953
  (707) 555-5943
  (e-mail address)

- Mr. Clayton Pearson
  Coach, Sonoma Soccer Club
  1330 Beringer Way, Penngrove, CA 94949
  (707) 555-9165
  (e-mail address)

- Ms. Joy Wershing
  Athletic Director, Laguna High School
  1501 Herringbone Drive, Petaluma, CA 94953
  (707) 555-3548
  (e-mail address)

Academic information

Providing academic information allows the coach to quickly qualify you as a student-athlete with at least the minimum qualifications to be considered for admission to his or her institution. It can also distinguish you from other interested student-athletes whose athletic talents may be similar to yours, helping the coach "sell" you to the admissions committee. Remember: You can't play for an institution unless you are first admitted.

One of the most commonly used indicators of your academic level is your grade point average. Make sure you list your most current GPA somewhere on your resume. We said earlier that you needed to have some idea of your GPA to assess your chances to go to college, so you may have this number readily available. If not, ask your guidance counselor or calculate it yourself from your grade reports. Avoid guessing, and never exaggerate your GPA.

"Be up front from the start. Your word is your honor," says Sam Koch, men's soccer coach, University of Massachusetts.

Although including your overall GPA is sufficient, you may choose to enclose a copy of your high school *transcript*. The transcript, which you can request from your school, generally is a record of all of your course grades from your freshman through senior years.

You also should include any standardized test scores, such as the SAT, ACT, PSAT or other academic test scores you feel are applicable. Like your GPA, these scores provide the coach a way to determine if you currently meet or are likely to meet in the future the institution's minimum entrance requirements.

Hopefully, you have been compiling any academic awards and honors you've received (for example, speech contest winner, student-of-the-month, dean's list, member of the honor society, class representative). Include a list of these awards in your resume, choosing what you believe to be the most important. It is best to list your more recent accomplishments, although showing a history of participation and honors can indicate strength in a particular area. Coaches tend to like leaders, so if you have held any leadership positions or offices, make sure these are listed. Just don't go so far back that the information is now irrelevant, such as Little League baseball captain or seventh grade class president.

Athletic information

Your athletic information should focus on what the coach is most interested in, such as the following:
- your physical dimensions
- relevant statistics for your sport
- accomplishments and awards, (MVP, #1 player on your high school team, team captain, etc.)
- the highest levels of competition in which you have participated, (regional teams, state or national ranking, etc.)
- any sports camps or showcases you have attended

If you have not already compiled this information, first brainstorm and write down everything you can think of. Then choose only the most current, most important and

Honesty is always best!

pertinent data. For instance, if you are sending your resume to the college baseball coach, you probably don't need to include your swimming record. However, showing your impressive speed in the 100-yard dash if you also run track is significant information for a soccer coach. If you are an athlete in more than one sport and you send out information to coaches of different sports, you need to tailor your Sports Resume Kit to reflect your abilities in each sport separately.

Make sure you always list your jersey number, if that is applicable to your sport. In that way a coach who comes to see you compete can identify you. If you have two different numbers, one for a high school team and one for a club team, list them both and indicate which is which.

Personal background

*Stand out from
other recruits*

Including some personal background information can help coaches remember you and gives them another way to distinguish you from other interested student-athletes. Extracurricular activities such as church group membership or volunteer jobs may signify to the coach that you are a caring individual and dedicated to something besides athletics. A well-rounded background generally impresses a college coach, and that versatility will definitely help you in the admissions process.

List of references

At the bottom of your sports resume include the names, addresses, telephone numbers and e-mail addresses of individuals whom the college coach can contact to get additional information about you. These individuals might be your high school and club team coaches, opposing team coaches or other college coaches you may know. It is a good idea to contact these individuals before you list them as references. This will give them an opportunity to think about what they will say on your behalf, so they won't be caught off guard when they are contacted. After you have sent your resume, you might even ask these same people to initiate contact with the college coach, by phone or e-mail, and give you a recommendation. At that time they can answer any questions the college coach has about you. Also, provide them with a copy of your resume so they won't forget to mention something important about you.

Letters of Recommendation

Letters of recommendation supply the college coach with the written opinions of others regarding your talents and abilities, and give insight into you as a person. Plan to include from one to three letters of recommendation in your Sports Resume Kit. One or two should be from coaches; others can be from a teacher, employer or family friend. These letters should attest to your ability, attitude and accomplishments, as well as your future potential.

Writing thoughtful letters of recommendation is a time-consuming process, so be considerate of the people from whom you request letters. Give each of these people a copy of your resume to use when writing your letter of recommendation and any other information about yourself that you want them to include. If possible, have them address each letter of recommendation to a specific coach. However, if this is too time-consuming, it's fine for them to address the letter "To Whom It May

Concern" and make and sign as many copies as you need. That way they will not have to rewrite or reprint the letter each time you need one. This will save you time as well, since it can be difficult to contact someone every time you need another letter

Not all letters of recommendation are equal. Some people you ask may think very highly of you but are unable to express themselves well in writing. This can be a problem because a poorly written letter or a letter that speaks only in the broadest generalities will not impress nor will it tell college coaches what they want to know about you. Try to pick people who will give you a positive recommendation (ask them!) and who can write well. We recommend that you ask for letters from more people than you think you will actually need, in case you have one or more letters that aren't useful.

Another thing you can do to help your letter writers is to let them know exactly what you are looking for. For example, "I would appreciate a letter of recommendation that includes:

- information about your relationship with me (coach, teacher, employer)
- the length of time you've known me (member of the varsity high school team for the past two years)
- information about your experience with me (besides being a student in my class, he was president of the Spanish Club while I was the club's advisor)
- your observations of my skills, abilities and attitudes that would help me succeed in the future
- your estimation of my potential in collegiate academics and/or athletics."

As mentioned earlier, it is best to plan ahead by giving your coaches or teachers ample time (one or two weeks is best) to write your letter of recommendation. Not only is it inconsiderate to pressure someone who is doing you a favor with a short deadline, but you might get less than a thorough recommendation if it is hurried. Tell your writers when you need their letters and how many copies you need. Either provide a self-addressed stamped manila envelope for mailing their letters to you or arrange a date and time to pick them up. Or have them e-mail you the letter. You can download it and send it by mail or e-mail it to the coaches. (A sample recommendation letter is shown on page 93 for one of the co-authors of this book, Todd Caven.)

Pick your strongest recommendations

MONTGOMERY HIGH SCHOOL

GARY MILES, Principal   ROBERT E. ACQUISTAPACE, Vice Principal
EVELYN N. TRUMAN, Assistant Principal   RICHARD E. STARR, Assistant Principal

1250 HAHMAN DRIVE   SANTA ROSA, CALIFORNIA 95405   (707) 528-5191

Dear Coach:

I have had the privilege of coaching against soccer and baseball teams on which Todd Caven participated for the past two years. During that time, I had the opportunity to observe him not only as an athlete but as a student as well.

Todd Caven is indeed a very fine athlete. He has excelled in both varsity soccer and varsity baseball during both his sophomore and junior year. In soccer, he was instrumental in leading his team to an undefeated season. In baseball, Todd has been one of the finest players in the league for the past two seasons. He is a fine young pitcher with great potential. He is also a good infielder who hits for a good average primarily because of his ability to consistently make contact regardless of the situation. Todd is definitely a hard working team player with a great deal of athletic potential.

Todd is not only a very fine athlete, he is also an outstanding student academically. He is one of the top students in his class and maintains high academic standards in a very demanding academic program. He is active in school activities as indicated by his being student body president at Santa Rosa High School next fall.

I have observed many personality traits that have accounted for Todd's success. He is hard working, dedicated, and dependable. He is constantly striving to make athletics a pleasurable experience for everyone involved. Todd is very highly respected throughout the community and the North Bay League.

In summary, I feel that Todd Caven would be an excellent addition to any school or athletic program. I only wish that I would have had the opportunity to coach this fine young man.

Sincerely,

Russ Peterich
Montgomery High School
Soccer and Baseball Coach

RP / lm

In Pursuit of Excellence

Sports Video

Videos showcase your talent

Mention a videotape or DVD in your cover letter, but do not send it with the Sports Resume Kit. Instead, include an offer to supply it to the coach upon request. When you are considering colleges outside your immediate geographical area, it is essential to have up-to-date game or event films to show prospective coaches who may be unable to see you perform in person. Because you don't yet know whether the coach wants a tape or what he or she wants to see (for example, full game, highlights or specific skills), state that you have film available and will send it upon request. By asking what the coach wants to see, you can better determine what he or she is looking for. You can then adapt the tape to fit the coach's needs.

A video helps equalize the recruiting game for student-athletes from rural communities or those located across the country from particular colleges or universities. Also, it allows out-of-state coaches who may not be able to watch you in person to see you perform without having to come to your area. If they like what they see, your tape might even persuade them to spend part of their limited recruiting dollars traveling to watch you play personally. Ask your high school or club coach to have videos taken of key games and ask for copies of all films. Again, be considerate and offer to provide a blank tape or DVD for your coach to use.

In case your sporting events are not taped, you need to arrange for videos to be taken, either by a parent, a friend or a professional videographer. Although hiring a professional can be expensive, one way to cut costs is to have the parents of team members pool their funds and hire a videographer, preferably one who specializes in filming sporting events.

The parents of a softball player on an eastern Montana high school team organized several other families and together they paid a videographer to film five games during her sophomore season and again in her junior season. Then each family had the tapes reproduced, and some families later edited them, depending on what each college coach wanted to see. Not only was this a relatively inexpensive way to get the tapes each family needed, but they had game films to enjoy for years to come.

Video or DVD? Ask the coach

Sometimes television stations tape local high school or community college games in their area. If this is true in your community, call and ask whether you can arrange to get copies of footage from those games.

Most coaches answered "yes" to our survey question, "Do you recommend that a student-athlete have a videotape or DVD prepared demonstrating his or her athletic abilities?" Some coaches said, "It depends" and went on to explain that they don't need to see a tape if they are able to see the athlete perform in person or if the sports statistics provide the information they need, for example, swimming or track times.

In general, the kinds of videotapes coaches want to see depend on which sport they coach and their personal preferences. The following reveals the variety of their responses:

"Film can spark our interest. Send a highlight tape, not the entire game; 15 minutes is enough," says Kim Sutton, women's soccer coach, CSU Chico, California.

"Keep it simple," says Lin Outten, men's soccer coach at Washington College in Maryland, "...not a highlight tape, instead send a complete game tape."

Jerry Snyder, softball coach, University of South Carolina at Aiken has special requirements: "I want to receive a well-made videotape using lots of angles and showing anything and everything that a student-athlete thinks the coach could possibly be interested in. Sell yourself on the tape."

Field hockey coach Beth Anders from Old Dominion University prefers "a game tape instead of isolated skills and drills," while Chris Bates, men's lacrosse coach at Drexel University in Pennsylvania, wants to see aggressive play: "...someone who wins face-offs or picks up a large amount of ground balls, etc."

Joan E. Powell, NCAA and United States Volleyball Association referee and former high school volleyball coach, recommends that the student-athlete "...introduce him- or herself at the beginning of a video. For example, 'Hi. My name is Mary Smith. I am a 5'9" junior at Coronado High School in Colorado Springs. I am a right-handed swing hitter with a 7'6" reach and a 24" vertical jump. My GPA is 3.25 and my SAT score is 998. What you are about to see is a skills tape followed by some game footage. I am starting in left front; my jersey number is 4.'"

Never send a master copy

As you can see, videotape preferences vary with individual coaches and the sports in which they are involved. This is why you need to ask a coach who requests a videotape just what he or she prefers to see:

- an entire game or event
- a highlight film
- an edited game film

Don't ever send your original videotape (master copy) or only DVD. Thirty-year high school volleyball coach Powell advises, "Make enough copies to send to college coaches, but not your original. Some coaches are good about getting the video back, others are not."

Game/Event Schedule

Because getting coaches to see you in action is extremely important, you should include your upcoming game/event schedule, with the date, time and location of each event, along with the name, phone number and e-mail address of your coach. Also, make sure you include your jersey number, either on the schedule or in the cover letter.

News Clippings

News clippings enliven your Sports Resume Kit. If you have been written up in your school or local newspaper for your athletic and academic accomplishments, include the articles.

Make a copy of each article, reducing it on the copy machine, if necessary, to make it fit an 8 1/2 x 11" or 8 1/2 x 14" piece of paper (make sure it is legible—not too dark or light). Include the source (for example, *Tri-City Daily Record*) and the date the article appeared. Highlight your name each time it appears in the article so the coach can easily find the section about you. Highlight copies rather than the original, since during copying highlighted words may darken or get blacked out altogether.

If you have several short write-ups, cut and paste them on a piece of paper to create a collage. Photocopy and then highlight your name in each article. You don't want to overwhelm the coach with so many articles that he or she cannot possibly read them all, so pick the best ones that show your most important accomplishments or best performances.

Your Picture

A picture is worth 1,000 words!

Send a picture of yourself along with your Sports Resume Kit. That way you become more than just a name, and it is easier for a coach to remember you. Generally, the best choice is a photo of you in your uniform, with the number of your jersey plainly visible.

Another idea is to have a picture taken of you in action. However, you will want it to be close-up enough to show your face, so the coach can recognize you. It won't help you to be pictured as a blur in the 100-yard dash or with a wave of water blocking your face during a swim meet. Either have reprints made of a good, clear photo or have a color picture photocopied. You may want to affix the picture to your sports resume so, when the coach is looking at your information, he or she can associate it with a face.

Putting It All Together

When all the components for your Sports Resume Kit are completed, assemble them in their order of importance. What you want the coach to see first should be at the beginning. The following is our suggested order:

- Cover letter
- Resume
- Letters of recommendation
- Game or event schedule
- News clippings
- Picture

Sports Resume Kit Tips

Here are more tips to help you:
- Put your name and page number on each page of your kit.
- Assemble your kit with a large paper clip or staples.
- Sign your cover letter.
- Make a copy of each letter.
- File the copies so you can retrieve them if necessary.
- Take one last look to make sure you have not forgotten anything.

E-mail or snail-mail? Ask the coach

Next, address a large manila envelope to the coach, write your return address on the left upper corner or back of the envelope, insert your Sports Resume Kit and mail it. Make sure you have sufficient postage by taking it to the post office or weighing it yourself if you have a postage scale. (Or go to the USPS.com website for mailing information.) Many coaches encourage potential recruits to e-mail their Sports Resume Kit. You might do that, and then follow up just as you will if you send the kit by mail, as explained in Chapter 9.

It is important to make a list of all the colleges where you send your Sports Resume Kit and to write down the date you sent the material. (See Materials Tracking Chart on page 162.) You should also mark this date on your calendar.

Remember, your Sports Resume Kit is your chance to make a good first impression on the coach. It should represent you at your best and show your desire to be part of the institution's athletic program. Just as you would dress neatly, comb your hair and talk politely when you meet the coach in person, so you want your correspondence to be well-written, neat and impressive.

Summary

⚽ The Sports Resume Kit is your sales or marketing package. It is your chance to show yourself in the best light possible.

⚽ A resume is a brief overview of your skills and accomplishments and is similar to what you compile when applying for a job. As the job resume is designed to impress a prospective employer, your sports/academic resume is designed to attract the interest of college coaches.

⚽ Letters of recommendation are extremely important; they should attest to your accomplishments and talents, as well as your potential for success in collegiate level athletics and academics.

⚽ Videotapes and DVDs of your athletic performance are beneficial to draw the attention of college coaches and to motivate them to see you perform in person. Rarely do coaches offer a scholarship to someone they have never seen compete.

⚽ The presentation of your Sports Resume Kit is important. A poorly executed, messy presentation is likely to turn off a college coach's interest.

In the next chapter we will talk about what to do after you send your Sports Resume Kit:
- **how to talk to coaches**
- **why following up with e-mails, phone calls and new information is important**
- **how to gauge the coach's level of interest in you**
- **how to successfully plan and carry out campus and home visits**

We will also give you some tips on what to do and what not to do in your communication with college coaches to help you win their confidence and ultimately, a sports scholarship.

Increase your Chances of Being Chosen

"If a recruit continually expresses and demonstrates genuine interest in our school, we will definitely follow up with a more intensive recruitment."

Greg Patton
Coach, men's tennis
Boise State University, Idaho

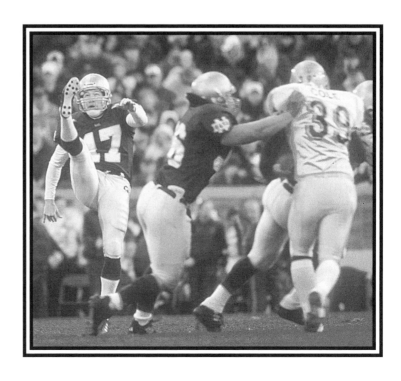

Importance of Following Up the Sports Resume Kit

Follow up with the coach

Wow! Don't you feel great? You sent off your Sports Resume Kit to the dozen or so schools that interest you most. You made a list of those schools and noted on your calendar the dates you sent your packets. So, now you can just sit back and wait for coaches to contact you or your high school coach, right? Not quite.

Now you need to follow up with the coaches to whom you sent your information. Wait a week or two from the date you dropped a Sports Resume Kit in the mail, and then call or e-mail each coach to confirm that your packet was received. You can say something like, "Hi, this is Jeff Jones from Newton, Illinois. I recently sent you my sports and academic history, and I'm calling to make sure you received it and see if you have any questions."

Following up will put you ahead of your competition—other student-athletes who also sent letters or e-mails but who may be sitting back and waiting for the phone to ring. Communicating directly with the coach can also give you a chance to ask questions and demonstrate that you are sincere in your interest. Don't leave anything to chance. Take the initiative by following up on the information you sent.

Markus Roeders, women's soccer coach at Marquette University, Wisconsin, has this suggestion: "The player should continue to initiate contact with the coach until he or she has received a reply."

The majority of coaches who took part in our survey responded favorably to student-athletes initiating contact with them to show their interest. In fact, an overwhelming 98 percent said they want to be contacted in writing or e-mail by student-athletes; another 83 percent said they also appreciate being contacted by phone.

Sam Koch, men's soccer coach, University of Massachusetts, states, "I want to help the student that is truly interested in our school. The more interest and incentive he shows us, the more we want to help him get the information he needs compared to someone who still has 25 schools on his list."

Keeping the Coaches Updated

Update coaches often

As the season progresses and events change or are added, such as an invitational tournament or a championship series, you need to update college coaches on your achievements. An e-mail, phone call, brief postcard or short letter is sufficient. This ongoing contact serves two purposes: to impart new information and to remind the coach about you. Any time new information becomes available, such as winning an award, breaking a record, increasing an event time, being elected team captain, etc., you should update the coaches in whose programs you are interested. Providing updates keeps you on the coach's mind and helps to distinguish you from the hundreds of other recruits the coach might be considering.

"Coaches are extremely busy and are contacted by hundreds of athletes each year. For her to make an impression, a coach may need to see or hear the athlete's name several times," explains Kim Sutton women's soccer coach, CSU Chico, California.

The Value of Persistence

Persistence, not pestiness!

Persistence, a trait common to successful people, is holding fast to a course of action or goal and refusing to be discouraged. Be persistent in making sure that a coach knows who you are and that you are interested in his or her program. Do college coaches value persistence in student-athletes? Read for yourself:

"Persistence indicates a desire to play. Many times desire outweighs ability."
Susan Montgomery, coach, women's basketball, Old Dominion University, Virginia

"The persistent athlete shows me he has a real interest in attending our school. This is important to me."
Randy Lein, coach, men's golf, Arizona State University

"Persistence often translates to confidence. Coaches like confident players."
Jovan Vavic, coach, men's water polo, USC, California

"There is value to the squeaky wheel in terms of reiterating interest. The time coaches have to evaluate talent is finite; you can't help but prioritize those you think are very interested first."
Shellie Onstead, coach, women's field hockey, University of California at Berkeley

"Persistence is a positive characteristic, one we look for when recruiting prospective student-athletes."
Richard Turner, coach, men's and women's swimming, University of Arkansas at Little Rock

"Persistence reflects desire and the ability to work hard."
Carolyn J. Condit, coach, women's volleyball, Miami University, Ohio

"Persistence is an important asset for a quality player. He or she will seek to improve and stay with it!"
Stan Morrison, athletic director, University of California, Riverside

"Persistence is good—to a certain point. Do not go overboard. Try to make it as easy as possible for the coach."
John McCormick, associate head baseball coach, Florida Atlantic University.

Being persistent should not be confused with being a nuisance. There is a fine line between them, according to coaches.

Telephone or E-mail: Which is Best?

Many of today's coaches are savvy computer users who welcome e-mail messages. If their e-mail addresses are listed on the college website, or if they correspond with you via e-mail following your initial contact letter, you may assume that they use e-mail as an acceptable recruiting tool. But, there are other coaches who still prefer mail and telephone contact. If coaches don't respond to your e-mail, send another e-mail by the end of the week. If there is still no response, do not assume they aren't interested in you; understand that they may not use e-mail. Although e-mail is usually an easier way for a student-athlete to follow up with a coach, you must find out how a coach prefers that you proceed.

Sam Koch, men's soccer coach, University of Massachusetts, says, "I like e-mail. I can read it and respond without worrying about the time difference. I do a lot of my e-mails at 5 am. I certainly couldn't call anyone at that hour."

Karen Stanley, women's soccer coach, Santa Rosa Junior College, California, says, "Players almost always contact me by e-mail. I very seldom get regular mail from recruits anymore."

"I prefer a letter, but I'm OK with e-mail...both should be sincere and well thought out. What's important is that they show me they're interested in my program," says Shellie Onstead, field hockey coach, University of California at Berkeley.

E-mail is faster

Calling College Coaches

When coaches encourage you to call them, it's understandable if you are hesitant or shy about making those calls. However, knowing what you want to say before you call can give you confidence. You may want to jot down a short script for yourself to start off your conversation. And if you have any new information for the coaches, write it down so you don't forget to update them.

If you are still nervous, role playing with a parent or friend may help. Play yourself and let your partner be the coach. Try to run through several possible conversations and practice your part.

After you have introduced yourself and asked whether the coach has received the information you sent, a sample dialogue might go like this:

Coach: "Sam who? What kind of information?"

Recruit: "Sam Reynolds from Baton Rouge. You sent me a brochure about your basketball program and a player profile sheet several weeks ago. I returned it, along with my sports and academic information, just last week. Do you remember receiving it?"

Coach: "Oh, Sam, sure. Now I remember. You're the 6'2" guard on Baton Rouge's team, right? I did receive your packet and was impressed with your academics as well as your basketball stats. Did you say you have a video you can send me? I'd like to see you play in person but don't know if I'll be able to."

Recruit: "Sure, I can send you a video, Coach Reed. I have several game films and one edited video of highlights. Which would you prefer?"

Another conversation might go like this:

Coach: "I don't remember receiving anything, Sam. When did you send it to me?"

Recruit: (You check your calendar or list.) "I mailed a packet (or sent it by e-mail) on September 14 that included my sports resume and several letters of recommendation, along with other information."

Coach: "I don't think I ever received it. Sometimes mail gets lost or misplaced in the athletic department. How about telling me a little about yourself right now? Then you could re-send or e-mail the information packet to me."

Remember, college coaches want to know about you and your talents. They do not

To call or not to call

want to overlook anyone. "I'm always looking for a diamond in the rough," says Shellie Onstead, field hockey coach, University of California, Berkeley.

Coaches need athletes to fill their rosters, and they cannot possibly know about all the qualified student-athletes out there. So writing, e-mailing or calling is not only perfectly acceptable but welcome. Keep notes of when you called and with whom you talked. If you need to re-send a Sports Resume Kit, do so promptly.

Other Ways of Increasing Your Chances

Have Your High School or Club Coach Call the College

Coaches we surveyed also said they appreciate calls or e-mails from high school and club coaches regarding potential recruits. They consider high school coaches to be extremely valuable sources of information. So, having your coach contact the college coach and give you a recommendation is a great way to increase your chances of being noticed. You may need to encourage your coach to make a call on your behalf, however. A number of student-athletes we surveyed said that their high school coaches contacted college coaches to endorse their abilities only after the student-athlete asked them to do so. When you ask, provide your high school or club coach with the college coach's name, e-mail address and phone number for their convenience.

Lin Outten, men's soccer coach, Washington College, Maryland, agrees: "The student-athlete should write the coaches a quality letter and have the club or state team coach call the university."

Prepare to Be Seen In Action

The main goal of sending your Sports Resume Kit and following up with phone calls, e-mails and letters is to get the coach to come watch you compete. Hopefully, then you can impress him or her with your skills and generate further interest. However, be prepared for a college coach to show up without warning at any one of your contests. Don't necessarily expect advance notification.

Play hard and focused each and every day. You may do this already, but if not, get used to it. You don't want to persuade a coach to come see you and then, when he or she does come, be unprepared, not focused and off your game. Assume that you have only one shot with a particular coach, who probably won't give you a second chance if he or she is not impressed the first time.

This point is emphasized by the recruiting experience of a former college student-athlete, who says, "I spent a lot of my time in my junior year of high school contacting coaches and sending information about myself to generate coaches' interest. I was hoping for a scholarship, and I knew I had to get them to come and watch me play if I was going to have a chance. Well, I had a few college coaches come and see me early on and express some interest, but the coach of the school I really wanted to go to never showed up. Or so I thought.

"In my senior year I received a letter from the school saying that they were sorry, but that they would not be awarding me a scholarship. I was surprised to hear from them at all, so I called and talked to the coach. I asked him how he could determine not to offer me a scholarship if he hadn't even seen me play. And that's when I found

Prepare to be seen!

out that he already had. Earlier in the year, I was playing in a game, lost my temper and was ejected from the contest. Guess what game the coach saw?"

College coaches are not only looking at student-athlete's skills but at their demeanor before, during and after the event. Sam Koch, men's soccer coach, University of Massachusetts, says, "We watch players warm up. We look at how they react to stress during a game, at their behavior toward their teammates."

Summer Sports Camps

Increase your chances to impress the coach

"Summer sports camps are a super opportunity to get to know athletes for a week and also to see them progress," says John Ross, men's tennis coach, Calvin College, Michigan.

Many colleges host summer or holiday sports camps for high school and younger student-athletes. Camps that specialize in specific sports can be a great way to meet a particular coach and to get a first-hand view of his or her coaching style. What's more, you will gain incredible exposure to the college program and allow the coach and his staff the opportunity to view your athletic skills on a day-to-day basis. In addition, camps provide excellent training and help in pointing out areas for improvement. For more information on camps offered in your sport, contact the athletic departments of the schools that interest you.

High-Profile Teams, Tournaments and Competitions

Another way to increase your chances is to compete where you know the coaches will most likely be. Try to determine where the best competition is and position yourself to be in the thick of it. Participate at the highest level possible (for example, the state or regional team, all-star competitions, invitational showcases). These are the levels where you'll get the most exposure to college coaches.

"Play on the best teams and in tournaments where there's mass exposure to college coaches," advises Kim Sutton, women's soccer coach, CSU Chico, California.

Additionally, try to get involved with an organization that travels to compete out of your geographical area on occasion. The more territory you cover, the better the chance that you will compete in an area where a college coach is watching. You will also display your talents to other coaches who may spread the word about you.

Large tournaments and competitions are excellent opportunities for coaches to see many potential recruits in one place. A coach would have to spend a great deal of time and money to see ten athletes compete individually, but, he or she has to make only one trip to a large tournament. Who knows? A college coach may come to a tournament to see another athlete and in the process discover you!

Recruiting Services

Today, there are many businesses that specialize in helping the student-athlete locate potential athletic scholarship opportunities. These *recruiting services* are operated by private businesses for a fee and may charge a student-athlete and his or her family up to $2,500 or more for their work.

Generally, a recruiting service compiles a one- or two-page profile of the student-athlete, which is similar to the sports resume, with athletic and academic statistics, a picture of the student-athlete and possibly a quotation from the high school coach. The recruiting service attempts to match student-athletes with a number of different athletic programs at various colleges and universities by mailing their profiles to collegiate coaches in their sport. Once the initial contact has been made with the profile, any interested college coach can contact the student, if recruiting rules permit, and begin the recruiting process. Fees increase with additional services.

What College Coaches Think of Recruiting Services

Our College Recruiting Survey revealed the following:

Recruiting services—
are they for you?

- Recruiting services are more often used by college coaches of smaller schools than by larger, more competitive schools.
- Some college coaches dislike recruiting service information because they feel it is impersonal and does not demonstrate a student-athlete's unique interest in his or her particular program.
- Some college coaches find recruiting service information very helpful in the recruiting process.
- Some coaches feel that the information does not help them because they are unsure about the credentials of the person qualifying the student-athlete as a candidate for a particular level of athletics.

Should You Use a Recruiting Service?

A recruiting service is a business; as such, you should qualify it as you would any other business. Ask questions, such as how long the service has been operating and what degree of success it has had. Ask for references. Get names of former and current clients and contact them to inquire about their satisfaction with the service. Call college coaches in your sport and ask whether they use recruiting services to find prospective student-athletes. Then, if you feel confident with the information you receive, you may want to consider signing up.

Should you choose to hire a recruiting service, we suggest that you use it in addition to preparing the Sports Resume Kit and following up with coaches. You still need to contact the coach through letters, e-mails and phone calls, and prepare a videotape if the coach requests one. The profile prepared by a recruiting service can be a helpful addition to the game plan we have laid out in this book.

TABLE 8: RECRUITING SERVICES: PROS AND CONS

Advantages

- Recruiting services can save you time and effort by providing easy access to a database with the names and contact information of college coaches in your sport and by sending your profile out for you.
- Most services distribute an attractive profile that includes pertinent statistics in your sport.
- Recruiting services may know of specific programs in your sport that are looking for student-athletes with skills similar to yours.
- A recruiting service may expose you to college coaches you might not have otherwise contacted.
- Recruiting services may provide the quickest way for you to disseminate your information in case you have started the process late in your high school career.

Disadvantages

- Recruiting services can be expensive.
- Profiles are generally sent out in mass mailings/e-mail mailings and are not personalized for any one coach.
- Profiles are often sent in groups consisting of many profiles of other student-athletes, making your profile easier to overlook.
- Recruiting services may charge an extra fee to update your profile.
- Since coaches are sometimes unsure of the credentials of the person qualifying the student-athlete, they may not find information from recruiting services helpful.

Visit the Campus

Campus visit: a must!

Visit campuses that interest you early in your high school years, if possible. Some student-athletes visit campuses with their parents or other students just so they can see the facilities and get a feeling for college life. Visiting a campus while school is in session is best because you can get the full flavor of a campus only when it is bustling with student activity. But if you cannot do that, a visit during summertime is better than no visit at all. Seeing the place where you might spend the next four or five years is preferable to arriving there ready to move into the dorm without having set eyes on the campus. You might be surprised and disappointed. Be sure to call the coach in advance to set up an appointment to meet while you're visiting the campus.

A college freshman who was offered a soccer scholarship at a small college across the country from her home decided to accept it even though she had not visited the campus. She was not offered an expense-paid recruiting trip, and her family did not feel they could afford to send her. She left for preseason practice in mid-summer and returned home several weeks later. She found the urban environment where the campus was located to be intimidating and did not care for her teammates or the coach. Had she visited the campus in advance, she might have realized that this was not an environment in which she felt comfortable.

A swimmer at a Division II school in Nebraska says, "Going to a college you've never visited before is like going on a blind date. You may like it or you may not. The difference is that you can go home after an evening with a blind date."

Official Campus Visits (Recruiting Trips)

Coaches who are recruiting you will usually invite you visit their campus. This is called an *official campus visit* or *recruiting trip*. Some, if they are seriously interested and their budgets allow, may offer you an expense-paid trip, called a *paid visit*. If the school is far away, this can be a real bonus because otherwise it might be difficult financially to make the trip. According to NCAA rules, you are limited to one official visit per college up to a maximum of five official visits to Division I or II colleges (paid or unpaid.) You may not take an official campus visit until the beginning day of your senior year. Any additional campus visits, called *unofficial campus visits,* must be at your own expense. So, you can visit a college campus at your own expense at any time and as many times as you like. You do not have to wait until your senior year.

Kim Sutton, women's soccer coach, CSU Chico, California says, "The majority of colleges do not have the budget for paid visits. We also don't have the personnel to go all over the country to recruit."

Compare campuses

Coaches and players agree that visiting the campus, whether an official or unofficial campus visit, is invaluable to the recruiting process, both for the student-athlete and the school. Campus visits provide an opportunity for you to experience the campus and meet and become acquainted with the coaching staff and your potential future teammates.

Chris P., a Stanford graduate and former varsity soccer player, advises recruits when visiting the campus to "...focus on the school. Try to interact with the students."

Sutton recommends that prospective student-athletes "always visit the campus and meet the players. Visit with an open mind, not just with scholarship dollars attached."

Sam Koch, men's soccer coach, University of Massachusetts, suggests, "Visit the schools you are interested in. Even when you think you might like one best, visit the others, too, so you can compare them before you make that commitment."

What to Expect on an Official Campus Visit

Never commit on a campus visit

Most campus visits arranged by the coach are well planned. Expect to stay with a team player in a dorm or apartment (though sometimes other arrangements are made). You most likely will meet with the coach several times over the course of your stay, so you two can get to know one another and ask questions. You probably will be introduced to most of the current players and may even get to see them compete if they are in-season. You also can expect to be taken to some social events, such as dinner, another sporting event at the college or a party. During the days you might go with various players to their classes so you can get a feel for what academic life is like at the school and to see the college facilities. Before you leave, you can almost be sure that the coach will ask you the question, "Well, what do you think?"

Geoff P., former kicker on the University of Washington football team reminisces about his recruiting trip: "I flew to Seattle and was met at the airport. They (the head coach and a player) took me out to a nice place for dinner the first night. Then the other player and I met a couple of other teammates, and they took me to see some of the city's night life. They really showed me a good time."

He continues, "The next day I had breakfast with an assistant coach and took a tour of the campus, met with an academic advisor, then went out to dinner with the coach and a couple more players. I felt important. I guess that's probably how they wanted me to feel."

Many student-athletes think it is crucial for recruits to explore all aspects of the school during any campus visit. Talk to nonathletes as you wander around. Find out how they like the school and try to determine their attitudes about athletics on their campus. The cafeteria or student union is usually a good place to meet students.

How to Get the Most Out of Your Campus Visit

Alexandra D., UCLA graduate and former women's volleyball player, tells about her recruiting trip to UCLA: "When I went for my campus visit, I was in awe. I didn't care about anything else except that I was at UCLA and proud of it! However, I know it's important to look at the campus surroundings, like housing, practice facilities, campus environment and surrounding town."

Although Alexandra was lucky and feels that she made the best college choice for herself, other student-athletes have been disappointed with specific aspects of college life that they never considered before they made their selection. They were so impressed by the attention they received on their recruiting trip that they failed to look realistically at the college and what it had to offer them besides the sport.

Dominic S., also from UCLA, and a former football player, offers this list of the most significant things to look for on a recruiting trip, beginning with the most important considerations:

Talk with prospective teammates

- Attitude and happiness of other athletes in the program
- Class type and size, school/campus site
- Living arrangements
- Typical daily sports schedule, both in-season and off-season
- Social atmosphere
- Athletic department educational resources—computer labs, tutorial programs, etc.

All college coaches are going to be concerned that you earn good enough grades to maintain your eligibility. After all, if you are on academic probation, you cannot compete. But you should also ask potential teammates about the coaches' (and athletic program's) overall attitudes towards academics. Ask the athletes as well about their classes to see whether they display an earnest attitude towards their education. If you are a serious student, it will be difficult to be in daily contact with teammates and coaches who do not encourage or respect that you are a student first, an athlete second—not the other way around.

Reflecting on her own experiences as a recruit, Jennifer P., former Division I women's soccer player, cites what she would look for if she were on a campus visit again: "I would definitely spend the majority of my time with the members of the team, not the coach nor the administration. You'll get your most important questions answered honestly by your potential future teammates. It's very important to find out how the coach treats the team and how he or she acts in stressful situations. Remember: coaches are trying to sell their school and program while recruiting—make sure you get the 'inside scoop' from the people he or she coaches."

Student-Athletes' Views on Campus Visits

The following recommendations are taken from a survey of student-athletes:

"Make it a point to observe how the athletes from the team interact with the rest of the student body. A great part of the college experience, even for the student-athlete, is based on diversity and the ability to interact with others who have different interests. Though your sport will be a large part of your college experience, it should not take away from the other aspects of life on campus."

"Get to know the coaches and players. If you are on the fence between two or more schools, the coaches and players can be the deciding factor. Make sure you can get along with the people you will be spending so much time with."

"Make sure you like the school. The campus, social life and students are all aspects you should take note of while on your recruiting trip."

"Talk to student-athletes in your sport about school. The emphasis of the trip will clearly be about the sport and the team. But ask about classes to get a feeling of how interested they are in the academics. Many top academic schools have student-athletes that could care less about school. This does not mean that you cannot be serious and take advantage of academic opportunities, but it is tough to compete both on the playing field and in the classroom if your teammates and coaches do not encourage and support academic excellence, or more importantly, respect the fact that you are a student-athlete, not just an athlete."

Make sure you like the school

"Get a 'feel' for the coach and his program. How does he perceive the direction that the program is taking? What are the ultimate goals for the program? How does he go about attempting to reach these goals? It's important to find out whether or not you will get along with the coach, since he will probably be the one constant in your four years of college life, and you will have at least as much interaction with him as any other person associated with that university. Make sure, as much as you can, that such an interaction will be a positive one."

"These are the most important things to look at when you're on a recruiting trip:
• Attitude of players toward their coaches
• Training, practice and playing facilities
• Attitude of other students toward their sport
• Social atmosphere of school
• Coaches' commitment to their program"

"Try to interact with the students. The best times you'll have will be with friends you make, not on the field."

"Find out what priorities your coach gives to academics and athletics. Also, ask other student-athletes how responsive the professors are about athletes having to miss classes or reschedule tests for road trips, games, etc."

"Meet and get to know your future teammates, as much as possible. Look at their lifestyles and how dedicated they are to winning. Nothing will be more frustrating for you than to give your all to winning, when your teammates are only concerned with the party after the game...or vice versa."

"It is important to meet and get to know some of the players. Feel out their reactions to you and yours to them."

Another student-athlete gives his most important list of questions for the recruit to ask himself or herself on the recruiting trip:
"Do I like the individual team members, not just the one the coach assigned to host me?

Is the campus a place where I think I'll feel comfortable spending the next four, or maybe five, years?

Are there things to do besides sports and study? Everyone needs a break sometimes.

Are the facilities good in terms of training, practices, etc. And are there other support staff (besides the head coach) to help off-season, like a weight trainer?

Did I have a fun time during the recruiting trip? Is this the kind of place I'd enjoy hanging out even without sports?

What are the other recruits like? Do I like them? It is important to like the players who will be starting out at your level. You will spend a lot of time with these people, especially as a freshman."

Act natural.
Be yourself.

Hosting Coaches in Your Home

A coach or recruiter who is seriously interested in you may want to visit your home and meet with you and your parents (and sometimes your coach). This could happen at the same time that the coach is in your area to watch you compete, or it could be a separate visit. Because of the cutbacks in coaches' recruiting funds, the home visit is not as prevalent as it once was and is often reserved for the blue-chip athlete. However, a coach or recruiter may call and ask to visit your home. While this is exciting, it can also strike panic into the hearts of many young student-athletes and their families.

One parent of a basketball player remembers, "For three days before the coach visited, we cleaned and polished everything. He was coming for dinner, so the whole family practiced table manners and wondered what we should talk about."

"Be yourself," advises California high school coach, Russ Peterich, who has been invited to sit in on home recruiting visits by a number of college coaches in his area. "Even though it may seem like a big deal, remember, the coach is visiting you because he or she is interested in you. Don't put on airs and try to be someone you're not. Act as natural as you can."

Thank-You Letters

Manners count:
Thank the coach

After you have visited a campus, been visited by a coach or recruiter or even carried on a lengthy telephone conversation with a member of the coaching staff, you should again follow up with an e-mail, short note or postcard. It doesn't have to be long or complicated. A "thank-you" for the home visit, information or campus visit is an excellent way to show your maturity and reaffirm your interest in the school. It also offers another opportunity for you to keep in contact with the coach.

A sample thank-you note might go something like the following:

Dear Coach Fry,

I enjoyed visiting Tall Timbers University and want to express my appreciation to you for coordinating all the weekend's activities and events. I especially liked staying in the dorm with Dave and Steve. They are great guys and introduced me to the campus and some other students. I also enjoyed meeting your assistant coaches and look forward to the possibility of playing for you in the future.

Thanks again,
Christopher Michaels

You could send a picture postcard from your city or state, which would be especially appropriate if the coach visited you at your home. A postcard is nice because its size limits how much you can write. The same message as above would be appropriate or something even shorter, such as:

Coach Stafford,

Thanks for visiting us last week. Your appearance at the meet was exciting, especially since I won the 100!! I enjoyed speaking with you and hearing more about your track program. I am very interested in attending State and look forward to hearing from you soon.

Sara Jones

If e-mail is more your communication style (and the coach's), send the same well thought out message via e-mail. Make sure spelling and punctuation is correct. Don't fall into the abbreviated syntax you use with friends. No "thnk U or CU soon."

Parents' Role in Recruiting

Involve your parents throughout the entire recruiting process. Next to you, they are the ones who will be most affected by the decisions made during this time, such as cost of school, distance from home, etc. But parents need to be in the background during the initial stages of recruiting. They should provide support and serve in an advisory capacity. You will want their input about where to look for a scholarship, how much tuition you can afford and what schools are the right ones for you.

Parents:
Your role is supportive

"The student-athlete, not the parent, should contact and correspond with the coach," says John Ross, women's basketball and men's tennis coach, Calvin College, Michigan. "The athlete needs to take the initiative."

When asked what role the parents of student-athletes should play during the recruiting process, most college coaches, while appreciating the importance of parents in the student-athletes' lives, prefer to deal only with student-athletes—at least at the initial recruiting stage—with parents generally remaining in the background. They overwhelmingly encouraged the student-athlete, rather than the parent, to take the lead. Since it is the student-athlete whom the coach will work with for four to five years, it is that individual the coach wants to become acquainted with during the recruiting period before making any type of offer.

"I can appreciate parents wanting the best for their child, but sometimes they are overbearing and don't realize that they're putting their son or daughter at a disadvantage," says Chris Bates, head men's lacrosse coach, Drexel University, Pennsylvania. "I want to hear a young man stammer through an introduction. I want him to advocate for himself. That's the young man I want to deal with."

An overzealous parent can block this interaction and even cause a coach to reject a student-athlete from the program. The coach may feel that the prospect of dealing with these parents the entire time the student is at school— "How come my son/daughter isn't getting more playing time?"—might be too burdensome.

Should a parent ever get involved with the coach directly? Yes. It is important that your parents become more active later in the process when you have narrowed your choices down to a few schools and have received scholarship offers. Because your parents most likely are the ones who will be paying for your college education, only they know what they can afford should the scholarship cover only part of your entire expenses. More on negotiating with coaches is found in Chapter 10.

Parents should also be part of a home visit by a coach, the signing of a letter of intent and possibly visits to campuses, although for an official campus visit, the student-athlete might want to go alone.

Nothing is worse for a coach than having to listen to parents go on and on about the accomplishments of their offspring and why their son or daughter should be offered a scholarship. This kind of interaction could have negative consequences.

Here are just a few tips coaches shared:

"I want to get a feel for the parents. It gives you a better idea about the kids. Sometimes the parents can be the deal-maker or deal-breaker for me," says Shellie Onstead, field hockey coach, University of California, Berkeley.

"Don't have your Dad do a 'voice over' on the video," advises Stan Morrison, director of athletics, University of California at Riverside.

"Make sure you carry your own suitcase and sports bag when you come for a campus visit. I'm really put off if I see your parents carrying them for you." says Sam Koch, men's soccer coach, University of Massachusetts.

From a consensus of college coaches interviewed and surveyed, we created the following list of what **not** to do during the recruiting process:

★

Pushy parents can hurt kids' chances

10 Ways to Turn Off College Coaches

1. Be dishonest: Lie about your grades, accomplishments or stats.
2. Focus only on what the college will do for you and ignore what contributions you can make to the college and the athletic program.
3. Boast and brag.
4. Play one school's program against another.
5. Show little or no regard for the academic side of college.
6. Look like a slob on your campus visit.
7. Fail to return applications or questionnaires as requested.
8. Pay little or no attention to the accuracy or appearance of your correspondence.
9. Have your parents call the coach on your behalf.
10. Show disrespect for the coach's time by arriving on campus without first calling for an appointment.

Summary

- Follow up with coaches after you send your Sports Resume Kit and whenever you have new information to offer. This reminds them about you and reaffirms your interest in their athletic program.

- Persistence on your part can make the difference between your being chosen or overlooked.

- Visit schools that interest you to get a feeling for the campus and the athletic program.

- Thank-you notes demonstrate your good manners, maturity and continued interest in the school.

- Parents are encouraged to play a significant supporting role in the recruiting process, letting the student-athlete take the lead.

You have now attracted the attention of college coaches by sending them your Sports Resume Kit and following up with phone calls, e-mails and letters to remind them about you and your interest in their programs. But what do you do next? How do you know whether all of the work you've done thus far has paid off? Chapter 10 tells you what to do when a scholarship offer is made and how to be successful as your own "sports agent."

10

What To Do When a Coach Is Interested

"Treat the college coach as your friend, not as an adversary. Through conversation, infor-mation-gathering and negotiation, the two of you will be able to come to a rational decision as to whether the school is the right fit for you."

Mark S.
Former player, men's soccer
Stanford University, California

What to Expect from Interested College Coaches

Recruiting is like matchmaking

Responses from college coaches who express interest in you may be varied. You might be receiving letters, e-mails or telephone calls from some coaches as soon as they are allowed to contact you, based on recruiting rules. More on recruiting rules is found in Chapter 11.

Other coaches will begin contacting the references you listed in your Sports Resume Kit, your high school or club coaches and any other sources they have in your area to get a better idea about your skill level. As we mentioned earlier, it is very rare for a student-athlete to be awarded an athletic scholarship without first having been seen by the college coach or a representative. Therefore, regardless of the approach, interested coaches will definitely want to see you compete so that they can make a final determination as to whether they will pursue you.

If coaches decide to recruit you further, they will start contacting you more frequently, giving you additional information about their athletic programs and school and asking you questions to gauge your level of interest. They will also try to discover how you might fit in with the other players, as well as the rest of the coaching staff. Additionally, they will be curious to know what other schools you are considering and whether you are being recruited by anyone else. In general, they will try to determine how much you want to go to their school and what they can entice you with to help persuade you to choose their program. They may also invite you for an official campus visit.

"UCLA's assistant coach contacted me and let me know they were interested in me and asked if I would like to come up to the school for a recruiting trip. It was very informal," relates Alexandra D.

"I was flown to the campus, put up with a few of the players and taken to a football and a water polo game. Afterwards, the coach took me out to dinner. It was a great feeling," remembers Chuck M.

As you continue through the recruiting process, it is important for you to understand that, just as you have been considering various colleges, coaches are considering many different student-athletes for sports scholarship offers. A college coach generally ranks prospective recruits in order of his or her preference and, as certain determinations are made about each player (for example, interest in program, chances of enrollment, attitude), these rankings change. Unless the coach is certain that you should receive a scholarship, he or she will wait until all determinations are made about student-athletes under consideration before making a scholarship offer. Just as you will be holding out to get into your first-choice school, the coach will be holding out for his or her top players.

In our survey of college coaches, three athletic factors were cited as most important in deciding which particular athlete should be awarded a scholarship:

- Athletic ability: Which player is the best?
- Program needs: Does the program need one particular type of athlete or skill more than another?

- Coachability of student-athlete: Can the student-athlete be coached or will he or she be more difficult to work with than someone else?

Receiving a Scholarship Offer

After a coach has thoroughly reviewed program needs and made the determination that your participation would benefit the program, a scholarship *offer* will be made to you, usually in a telephone call from the coach. At this time, you will probably be very familiar with the coach, as you will have spoken and been in e-mail contact often throughout the process.

Here are a few comments from former collegiate athletes about their experiences:

"I was offered several scholarships during the national football recruiting period, which was before I was admitted to any of the schools. I believe they were contingent upon my being admitted to the institutions."

"I received early admittance sometime in January and received my scholarship offer at the end of January. I was number four on a list that would make three offers; so I had to wait and see if one of the top three candidates chose another school."

"I don't remember exactly, but I believe the coach informed me that they were offering me a scholarship before I was accepted. We did not speak specifically about the amount until after I was officially accepted."

"I was offered my athletic scholarship during spring of my senior year in high school, just prior to receipt of my acceptance letter from the college."

"At the time, water polo did not have early admittance. I found out I was accepted to the school, visited the campus that week and was offered the scholarship at the end of the trip."

"The scholarship was offered before my admittance to the school, and, after my admittance became known to the athletic office, it was formalized in a letter of intent. The letter of intent only covered that year, and each year for three more years, I signed another one."

"The coach called and confided in me that I was going to be getting a letter of acceptance. I knew that he was offering me a scholarship; we had already negotiated the amount. But it was dependent on my being accepted and it wasn't put in writing until after my acceptance."

Once you receive a scholarship offer, you should have an idea of how much additional financial aid you will need to attend that school. If the offer is not enough, you need to let the coach know and then negotiate a higher award, if possible.

College athletes speak to recruits

How to be Successful in Your Negotiations with Coaches

Parents' Involvement in the Negotiation Process

★

Get parents' help in negotiating

Up to this point in the recruiting process, parents have been urged to take a supporting role. Now, however, when it's time to deal directly with the coach or recruiter and decide which school is offering the best scholarship and other benefits, parents should assume a more visible, prominent role. The student-athlete often needs strong representation when *negotiating* with an experienced college coach.

Some parents, however, often feel inadequate when they find themselves thrust into the role of "sports agent." One mother says, "I was surprised when I realized I was being called upon to negotiate with college coaches. I wish I had been more prepared."

Another parent wishes he had known someone knowledgeable to talk to, someone who had gone through the process before he and his daughter did. Talking to other parents of collegiate student-athletes is a good idea. Ask about their son or daughter's recruiting experiences and about their perception of the negotiating process.

When coaches come calling, it's something like a courtship. They phone and send you e-mails and notes through the mail. They invite you to visit their campus. They want you to choose their school over any other and will try to impress you, sometimes promising you favors they are not able to deliver. They may also, at this time, attempt to impress your parents, seeking their blessings and support for the "marriage" between you and their school.

This kind of attention is exciting, a boost to the ego, and even the most practical student-athlete might be tempted to succumb to the first offer, asking only, "Where do I sign?" The involvement of your parents should provide the level of clear-headedness necessary to balance the heat of the recruiting courtship. Like matchmakers, your parents will be the go-betweens, the negotiators of the alliance. Remember: Asking questions and understanding the answers you receive is the key to making the best decision. The following tips have been compiled with the help of many student-athletes, parents and college coaches:

Do's and Don'ts for Successful Negotiating

Do
- Determine what is most important to you.
- Talk to college student-athletes; ask direct questions.
- Be prepared to compromise.
- Observe how the coach talks about and treats his or her other players.
- Talk to the coach enough times to get an intuitive feeling about him or her.
- Ask yourself whether the coach has your best interests in mind.
- Base your final decision on facts, not fantasy.

Don't
- Play games; be honest about your needs.
- Be so shy that you forget to ask questions.
- Be so excited that you don't listen to the answers.
- Accept gifts, money or special favors.
- Be naive; do get all offers in writing.
- Overestimate your value, but don't underestimate it either.
- Be afraid to say no.

How to Negotiate

Negotiation is the art of talking over issues and arriving at consensus. Successful negotiation results in a conclusion where everyone concerned feels like a winner. Before negotiating with the coach, ask all your questions, listen to the coach's answers and ask questions of others, too. In other words, you have to do your homework. Do not depend solely on the coach's word. He or she may exaggerate the strengths of the program while minimizing any weaknesses. What you discover by talking to others may either corroborate or contradict the coach's statements.

Talking $$ with coaches

When it comes time to negotiate, listen carefully so that you understand what the coach is offering. Then either you or your parents should restate the proposal as you understand it and ask for clarification, if needed.

Parent: "I believe you said that John will get a 50 percent scholarship. Does that mean 50 percent of his total educational expenses or 50 percent of his tuition? And this is for one year only?"

Coach: "The 50 percent athletic scholarship covers 50 percent of John's tuition. Yes, I can only offer him a one-year-at-a-time scholarship. However, athletic scholarships are renewable for four years, and I don't see any reason why John shouldn't qualify."

Parent: "What exactly does he have to do to qualify?"

When the offer is not quite what you think it should be or enough to allow you to attend that school, discuss the issue with the coach.

Parent: "Tuition at Big Top U is $7,000, so 50 percent is $3,500. But his total expenses (room and board, books, supplies, etc.) including round-trip travel two times across the United States (in the fall, home and back for Christmas and return in the spring) is estimated at $18,000. It would be less costly for us if he were to go to State U because then his travel expenses would be negligible."

Coach: "I'll try to find another $1,500 to make up for his travel expenses." Or: "I can come up with another $1,000, which won't quite cover it but will help out."

Negotiation is an art!

The art of negotiation is a delicate one, and it takes a fine sense to know when the coach has offered all he or she is going to. Most importantly, you have to know whether you can afford to go to the school with the scholarship amount the coach offers. Sometimes coaches will add to the amount of scholarship dollars during the athlete's years at the college, but neither you nor your parents should count on that. Be honest about your situation and tell the coach exactly how much you need to go to the school.

Sam Koch, men's soccer coach, University of Massachusetts, gives this advice to student-athletes: "Be honest about your interest in a specific institution...be straightforward with coaches. Tell them for example, 'You are my number 3 choice out of five schools' or 'you are my number 1 choice, but I need $8,000 to attend your school.' Be specific."

One parent of a collegiate student-athlete remembers telling a coach, "The way your offer stands now, Shawn will probably not be able to go to your school, even though you're definitely his first choice."

"How much more would he need?" the coach asked. "Another $2,000 a year," the parent replied.

The next day the coach called back and offered $1,000 more in additional athletic scholarship dollars, with another $500 academic scholarship and $500 for work-study (a part-time job). The coach was able to put together the additional funds needed, though they were not all in the form of an athletic scholarship.

In this case, Shawn's mother was able to negotiate for a larger award by being straightforward about her family's needs, and the coach was able to meet those needs by combining money from several sources. The outcome was definitely a win-win result for both the coach and the student-athlete. More information on financial aid is found in Chapter 12.

The first offer is not always the last

It can be easier to negotiate if you have more than one scholarship offer. While you obviously have more to consider with multiple offers, you may be able to afford to take a stronger stance. A West Coast volleyball player was offered scholarships from three different university athletic programs. The school he chose ultimately doubled its original offer to encourage him to sign its letter of intent. This example shows that you should not assume that a coach's first offer is the last.

Whittle down your college list

When you are being recruited by more than one coach, you need to further compare colleges and their athletic programs. You should have already established a firm understanding of what each school has to offer in the earlier stages of the selection process. But, now that you may have whittled your list down to a few schools, you need to really focus on the areas that matter to you most. Below are questions to consider asking before making any decisions.

Considerations in Choosing Among Offers

Academic Program

- Does the school have the academic curriculum I want?
- Are courses available in my major areas of interest?
- How challenging is the school's academic program?
- Will it be difficult for me to keep up scholastically and remain eligible for my sport?
- What academic support is available?
- Is free tutoring available for student-athletes?
- Are specially trained academic/athletic advisors assigned to players?
- What other academic support services are available for student athletes?
- Are faculty members responsive to the special needs of student-athletes who may have to miss classes because of athletic competitions?
- Are practices or games scheduled during final exams?
- What is the graduation rate and grade point average for athletes in my sport?
- What is the graduation rate for all student-athletes at the college?
- What percentage of athletes graduate in five years?
  (See the NCAA's annual graduation report on www.ncaa.org, which shows the percentage of recruited athletes on athletic scholarships who graduate within

five years from the college.)

- What are the criteria for remaining academically eligible to participate in my sport?
- What will happen to my scholarship if I am placed on academic probation?

Athletic Program

- How do I qualify for the team? Do I have to try out?
- Is the team in a conference or a league? Which one(s)?
- How competitive is the conference/league as measured on a national level?
- Against which colleges does it compete?
- What is the expected time commitment to my sport?
- How many months of the year will we practice/play?
- How many hours per day/per week will I be expected to devote to the sport?
- What is the length of the season?
- What will my time commitment be during the off-season?
- What is the team's travel schedule?
- What methods of transportation are used for team travel? Who picks up the costs?
- What background and experience does the head coach have?
- What is his or her coaching philosophy and style of coaching?
- How do I think I would fit in, considering all these factors?
- If I sustain an injury that keeps me from participating in my sport, will my athletic scholarship continue?
- If my injury permanently sidelines me, will my scholarship be taken away? (NCAA rules prohibit colleges from cancelling because of injury.)
- What about an injury off the field?
- If it takes me five years to complete my degree, will I still get my scholarship money for the fifth year even though I've used up my four years of eligibility?
- What assurance do I have that the athletic program is financially strong?
- Is my sport given respect and sufficient financial support within the athletic program?
- Are the athletic department's expectations of student-athletes spelled out in writing and given to student-athletes?
- What is the substance abuse policy at the institution? Does drug testing take place?

The Scholarship

- What, if any, athletic scholarships are offered in my sport?
- How much of the total cost of attendance for this college does the scholarship cover?
- Is additional financial aid available?
- What is the balance my family is expected to pay?
- If the cost of tuition, room and board increases from year to year, does the scholarship also increase proportionately?
- What criteria are used to renew the scholarship each year? (Remember, scholarships are awarded only one academic year at a time.)

- Can the coach refuse to renew because I am not living up to his/her playing expectations? He or she wants to give the scholarship to another player? A new coach takes over the program and wants to clean house?
- Does the school provide a written contract stating the amount, duration, conditions and terms of the scholarship?
- If I decide I do not want to continue playing my sport, do I have to give my scholarship money back?

The College Rating Sheet

Never sign on a recruiting trip!

Developing a rating sheet for colleges that are recruiting you helps to identify factors that are important to you as you critique different programs. Ryan O., former Division I volleyball player says, "Having a system can help you put what is important to you on paper and is an excellent way to analyze different schools' strengths and weaknesses systematically."

The College Rating Sheet has been developed to assist you with making your decision. Follow the instructions for completing these sheets (See the completed College Rating Sheet on page 124. A blank rating sheet can be found on page 161 and on our website: www.winasportsscholarship.com.) Make as many copies as you need to rate all your colleges.

Although the College Rating Sheet can be a useful tool to help you organize your thoughts and ultimately reach a decision, it is only as good as the information you put into it. If you do not carefully think about the ratings you give, the total scores you end up with will be meaningless. So, make sure you have every bit of information you need to make an informed decision.

Chuck M., former Division I water polo player, advises, "Never make your final decision until you have evaluated all of your options. Then sleep on it. And, never, NEVER sign at the campus on a recruiting trip."

How To Fill Out the College Rating Sheets

Filling out the College Rating Sheet can be broken down into steps.

STEP 1: List all the factors that are important to you in selecting an institution under the "Factors to Consider" column. An easy way to organize your thoughts is to first list the academic and general factors that you believe are most important and then to list the athletic factors. Below are some suggestions of factors that you may want to consider. However, if other issues are important to you, feel free to add them.

Academic and General Factors

Location

Cost

Academic reputation

Size of student body (enrollment)

Academic facilities

Availability of housing

Availability of your major area of interest

Availability of classes

Student to teacher ratio

Social atmosphere

Coed or single sex

Extracurricular opportunities

Athletic Factors

Availability of scholarships

Athletic facilities

Game/event schedule

Coaching staff

Coach's interest

Teammates

Athletic department's commitment to program

Training schedule (in-season and off-season)

Expected amount of playing time

Potential of program success

STEP 2: Rate the importance of each factor from 1 (least important) to 5 (most important). These ratings should be written in under the column headed "Importance." This will help you weigh the factors that are most important to you.

STEP 3: List the schools you are considering across the tops of the columns (see the College Rating Sheet example on page 124). The College Rating Sheet has limited space, so if you have more schools than there is space, you can photocopy the sheet.

STEP 4: Rate each factor you have listed from 1 to 5 for each school you are considering, with 5 being the highest or most desirable and 1 being the lowest or least desirable.

For example, if the location of the school is important to you, and you want to attend a school in a rural setting, an institution located in the countryside may merit a

College Rating Sheet
(Rate each Institution 1-5, 5 being highest)
Name of Institution

Factors to Consider	Importance (1-5)	STATE U.		ROCKWELL ST.		BIG TOP COLL.		ACORN U.	
Location	3	x 2	6	x 3	9	x 4	12	x 1	3
Cost	4	x 1	4	x 4	16	x 2	8	x 3	12
Academic Reputation	4	x 5	20	x 2	8	x 4	16	x 1	4
Size of Institution	2	x 4	8	x 2	4	x 4	8	x 1	2
Housing Availability	3	x 4	12	x 2	6	x 3	9	x 3	9
Availability of Major	4	x 5	20	x 5	20	x 5	20	x 1	4
Avail. of Scholarships	5	x 1	5	x 4	20	x 3	15	x 5	25
Facilities	3	x 3	9	x 4	12	x 5	15	x 2	6
Competitiveness	3	x 2	6	x 3	9	x 2	6	x 4	12
Chances of playing in 1st year	4	x 4	16	x 2	8	x 4	16	x 3	12
Coaching Staff	4	x 2	8	x 2	8	x 5	20	x 5	20
Social Atmosphere	2	x 3	6	x 5	10	x 4	8	x 2	4
TOTAL			120		130		153		113

5 for you, while a school located in the middle of a large city may merit a 1.

Each space under the headings where you have listed your schools is divided into two columns. You will want to place your rating for each factor in the left column under the corresponding school. For example, on page 124 State U. has been given a rating of 2 for location. Rockwell State has been given a rating of 3, and so on. After you have rated each factor for each school, you are ready to calculate the result.

STEP 5: Calculate the results for each school. If you have done Steps 1-3 correctly, there should be one blank column for each school. In this blank column you will place the total score for each factor. Start with the first school listed. Multiply the rating given to the first factor by the rating giving for its "importance." The result of this multiplication should then be placed in the first blank space under the school for the factor.

For example, in the filled out College Rating Sheet location was given an importance rating of 3 and for State U. a rating of 2 was given for location. Therefore, in order to get the score for location for State U, we simply multiplied 3 x 2 = 6. To calculate the score for cost for State U, we multiplied an importance rating of 4 by a rating of 1, which equals 4, and so on until we had each factor score calculated for State U. Then move to your second school and repeat with the ratings you have given for every factor for that school.

After each factor score has been calculated, add up the scores for each school and write in the amount at the bottom of the column. For State U. we added up its factor score column (6+4+20+8+12+20+5+9+6+16+8+6) to get 120. Place the total factor score in the "total" row under the factor score column for each school.

STEP 6: Interpret the results. Once you have made all of the calculations and have filled in the total factor scores for each school, it is easy to see which school ranks highest in terms of what factors are important to you in choosing a school. The higher the score, the closer the match with your important factors. On the College Rating Sheet, Big Top College, with 153 points, received the highest score.

Get The Offer In Writing

An offer from the college must be in writing to be valid. Once you and your future coach have come to an agreement on the particulars, the coach or an athletic department representative must put the offer in writing and sign it. After you and your parents have read and made sure you understand the agreement, you are expected to sign and return it to the coach.

A current trend in some sports and at some schools is for coaches to make verbal offers to student-athletes before the *National Letter of Intent (NLI)* can be signed, and ask them to reciprocate (commit verbally). Although this approach is intended to speed up the recruiting process and sometimes may seem a relief to select high school players who are being bombarded with attention, you should keep in mind that the offer is not legally binding—on either the coach, the school or the student-athlete—unless it's in writing.

Rate scholarship offers

Always get the offer in writing!

National Letter of Intent (NLI)

The National Letter of Intent is a standard form of written agreement between the student-athlete and the college. It is used by many but not all Division I and II NCAA institutions. It specifies a time period during which prospects can sign their letters. This period varies from sport to sport but the early signing period is usually at the end of that sport's high school season.

You may sign only one NLI, and signing it commits you to enroll in a certain institution and play a specific sport. The NLI describes obligations and responsibilities to which you agree. Make sure you read it over carefully before signing. You, your parent or guardian and the athletic director of the institution must sign the NLI in order for it to be official. A sample National Letter of Intent is shown on pages 166-169.

How and When to Respond to Offers

While the National Letter of Intent has a specific time period during which you must respond, institutions that do not subscribe to the NLI will make their own written offers, and you must follow their deadlines and instructions. Ask the coaches who are recruiting you whether they use the NLI or another form of written agreement.

Summary

- Student-athletes and their parents must exercise a clear-headed approach to dealing with scholarship offers from college coaches.

- Although parents should stay in the background until scholarship offers are being discussed, at that point they must step forward into the role of "sports agent" to negotiate with coaches and help their son or daughter weigh offers from different institutions.

- Ask questions that will help you compare the academic and social environment, value of scholarships and the athletic programs at colleges that make offers.

- A rating sheet helps you to systematically compare colleges, using the information you have gathered.

- Negotiating with coaches can feel overwhelming unless you are prepared. Decide what's most important to you and how much scholarship aid you need (or are willing to accept.) Be honest and up front about your needs with the coach.

- Do not count on verbal promises; get all offers in writing. The National Letter of Intent, used by most colleges, spells out the offer in detail.

In addition to understanding how to negotiate, knowing the rules can help you to spot recruiting violations and save you from losing your eligibility. In Chapter 11 you will learn how to determine whether you are being illegally recruited and what to do about it. ▮▮▶

Illegal Recruiting Can Cost You: Know the Rules

"NCAA rules strictly prohibit colleges from speaking with prospective student-athletes until July 1 following the completion of their junior year of high school."

Kevin R. Price
Associate Director of Athletics-Compliance
Oregon State University

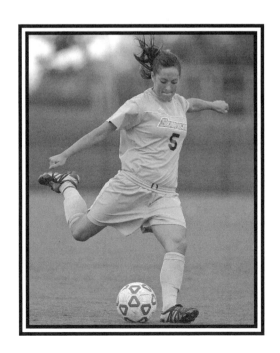

Recruiting Rules Protect Athletes

Recruiting rules are meant to protect you, the student-athlete. They are not meant to intimidate or entrap you. This book is NOT meant to be an authoritative source on recruiting regulations or athletic association rules. Rules are regularly updated or changed, so check the current publications from the NCAA (National Collegiate Athletic Association) and the NAIA (National Association of Intercollegiate Athletics), and talk to the individual schools.

Stories abound about superstars who play college sports but can barely read and athletes who exhaust their college eligibility but never graduate. Rules to protect the athlete from being exploited in these ways also apply to the recruitment of high school athletes. Regulations have been strengthened to encourage colleges to recruit only bona fide student-athletes, those who can compete academically as well as athletically.

Critics maintain that recruiting violations still occur, and that athletes who are ill prepared for success at the college level are still admitted by institutions eager to win a national championship. However, it is generally the blue-chip athlete or superstar, rather than the better-than-average athlete, for whom recruiters circumvent the rules. The dealings of overzealous recruiters have mandated tough regulations to keep recruiting honest. Remember, recruiting rules were created for your benefit. While they may seem rigid and restrictive, they are meant to protect you from being pestered and coerced by fiercely competitive recruiters.

Because the recruiting process is highly regulated by all of the national associations, coaches are very cognizant of the "do's and don'ts" of recruiting. If they are caught violating the rules, they run the risk of their program being put on probation, losing scholarships either temporarily or permanently and even being barred from intercollegiate competition for a period of time. Failure to follow the rules can cause you, the student-athlete, to be ineligible to compete in intercollegiate athletics.

A word of warning here about protecting your amateur status: Athletes can be considered amateurs only if they do not accept payment of any kind for their participation in athletics. If you or your parents accept money or gifts from a representative of a college athletic department or alumnus or booster, you can lose your amateur status and be declared ineligible to participate in college athletics.

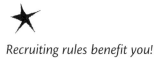

Recruiting rules benefit you!

The NCAA

Each of the divisions within the National College Athletic Association (NCAA) has slightly different rules, making it difficult for the recruit to know about or understand these differences. Yet, as complicated as NCAA rules appear to be, the student-athlete needs to understand enough to stay out of trouble and avoid any possible recruiting violations. The NCAA publishes a booklet, *NCAA Guide for the College-Bound Student-Athlete*, which is updated yearly, to help explain the rules. Your high school counselor may have these booklets available. You can also view and download the Guide from the NCAA website (www.ncaa.org) or request a free copy from the NCAA, P.O. Box 6222, Indianapolis, IN 46206-6222; (317) 917-6222.

Other Athletic Associations

The National Association of Intercollegiate Athletics (NAIA), an association of over 300 four-year colleges, has a similar publication, *A Guide for the College-Bound Student-Athlete.* Single copies can be downloaded from www.naia.org or requested from the NAIA, 23500 W. 105th St., Olathe, KS 66061; (913) 791-0044.

The National Christian College Athletic Association (NCCAA) is an association of 100 four-year Christian-based colleges. Contact the organization at www.thenccaa.org or write to 302 W. Washington St., Greenville, SC 29601. Call (864) 250-1199 for information.

The National Junior College Athletic Association (NJCAA) is the largest association of two-year colleges. Not every two-year or community college is a member; some conferences and states belong to their own associations. Talk to coaching personnel at community colleges that interest you to find out to which association their school belongs. The NJCAA has a recruiting guide called the *NJCAA Prospective Student-Athlete Brochure*, which is available by contacting the association at www.njcaa.org or writing to 1755 Telstar Dr., Ste. 103, Colorado Springs, CO 80920. You can also call (719) 590-9788 for information.

Athletic Conferences

Most colleges belong to athletic conferences, such as the Pac-10 and Big 10, that are usually geographically based groupings of schools. Some of these conferences have their own set of regulations in addition to their athletic association rules. Talk to the athletic director or coach at colleges that interest you or contact the athletic conference directly to request specific information.

Recruiting Rules

There are very strict regulations regarding the interaction between college coaches and high school student-athletes.

Restrictions on Contacting Students

You can initiate contact

According to the NCAA, a college coach is allowed to contact you in person off the college campus only after July 1 following completion of your junior year in high school. Additionally, neither a coach nor an athletic department representative may contact you by telephone until after this date, with a few exceptions for certain sports. Therefore, you are allowed to become a recruited student-athlete only after that time. See the latest *NCAA College-Bound Student-Athlete Guide* for more information.

Although a coach is not allowed to contact you in person or by phone prior to July 1 following completion of your junior year, recruiting letters from college coaches, faculty members and students are permitted on or after September 1 at the beginning of your junior year in high school. Because this is 10 months earlier than a coach can contact you in person, you might get letters of interest and general information about colleges from coaches during the 11th grade. But before that date, a coach cannot write, call, e-mail or talk to you away from the college campus. So if you send your initial contact letter and/or your Sports Resume Kit before September 1 at the beginning of your junior year, and you don't hear back from the coach right away, understand that the coach is just following the rules.

Sending initial letters of interest is standard practice for colleges. Student-athletes who receive them should not assume that they are actually being recruited. Many institutions, especially in Division I, send out hundreds of initial contact form letters to athletes who have been called to their attention in some way—either by college recruiters, recruiting services, scouting reports or by the athletes, their high school coaches or parents. This kind of letter indicates precursory interest only and means that the college coach would like to know more about you or whether you are interested in the school. Included with their initial letter is usually a form for the student-athlete to fill out and return. Once the coach has received more information, such as year, academic and athletic skill levels, he or she may or may not contact you again.

Nothing in the rules prevents you from contacting a coach by phone, e-mail or face-to-face on the college campus. You are allowed to write, e-mail or call anytime, as long as it is at your expense. The same is true of campus visits. You may visit a college campus and athletic facility anytime at your own expense. We point this out to let you know another good reason for you to take the initiative to contact coaches at colleges that interest you by letter, e-mail, telephone or by visiting the campus as soon as possible. You can do this any time. If you do not contact them first, they cannot contact you personally before July 1 following completion of your junior year.

Even after the July 1 rule, a coach can call you only once a week. A solution for the "one phone call per week" rule is that the student-athlete call the coach. Stan Morrison, athletic director, University of California, Irvine explains: "There is no restriction on the number of calls a prospect can make to a coach, but be judicious with your calls. Have a reason for calling. Perhaps you need a clarification of a recruiting rule, for example."

When a college coach comes to an athletic competition or practice in which you're participating to assess your abilities, it is called an *evaluation.* Coaching staff members may evaluate you no more than seven times in your senior year (except for women's basketball—five times, and football—six times) Tournament play on consecutive days counts as one evaluation. Any face-to-face meeting between you (or your parents) and a college coach, with any more conversation than "hello" passing between you, is called a *contact.* In all sports other than football, coaches are allowed to contact you in person off the college campus no more than three times during your senior year. In football and basketball there are specified time periods for evaluations and contacts.

Coaches are very careful to avoid wasting their contacts. That's why they might be curt or virtually ignore you if you try to speak to them away from the college campus before NCAA rules allow contact. Such behavior does not mean they are angry or uninterested; it just means they are being careful and will contact you personally when the time is appropriate.

Phone calls, e-mails, evaluations: Know the rules!

Official Campus Visits

During your senior year in high school, beginning the opening day of classes, you may take only one expense-paid (official) visit to any one campus. You are allowed a maximum of five expense-paid visits to college campuses. Rules for your visit are strict and include the following:

- Your visit may not exceed 48 hours.
- Expenses are paid only for you and your parents.
- What constitutes a legitimate expense, such as travel, lodging and meals, is strictly spelled out.
- Special privileges are limited.

Most everyone involved in college athletics agrees on the importance of visiting colleges for recruits. Trying to imagine what a school is like just by talking to the coach or seeing college catalogs and websites can be dangerous. Not every recruit is offered an expense-paid visit, and if you don't receive one, you should not feel slighted. The reason may be as simple as a lack of athletic department funds. If you can afford it, you should consider paying for the trip yourself, as this may be your only option.

Know the Rules: It's Your Responsibility!

Although recruiting rules and regulations can be complex, it is your responsibility to make sure you are not involved in anything that might jeopardize your eligibility during the recruiting process. Because the various athletic associations and conferences, and even the colleges themselves, may have slightly different rules, you should check with the college or athletic association when you need rule clarification. After all, one little mistake could cause you to be unable to compete in your sport at the collegiate level.

Warning Signs of Illegal Recruiting

- A member of a college coaching staff approaches you at one of your athletic events and talks to you before July 1 following completion of your junior year.
- A member of the coaching staff or a student-athlete contacts you by phone or e-mail about enrolling in their college athletic program prior to July 1 of the completion of your junior year.
- An alumnus, booster or college representative tries at any time to talk you into playing a sport at their college.
- You or any member of your family is offered money, gifts or special privileges by representatives of a college or its athletic department.
- You are offered more than one expense-paid visit to a single college campus.
- You are promised a four-year scholarship or offered money over and above the amount of your specified college expenses by a coach or a representative of an institution's athletic interests.

What to Do if You Suspect You Are Being Illegally Recruited

If any of the preceding events happens or if you have concerns about the legality of any recruiting activity, you should immediately talk to the head coach of the collegiate athletic program or contact the athletic association to which the college belongs.

Summary

⚽ Strict regulations for the recruitment of student-athletes and intercollegiate athletic associations govern the conduct of member colleges in many areas, including recruiting.

⚽ Understanding what constitutes illegal recruiting can be challenging because of the different rules among athletic association divisions.

⚽ To clarify any recruiting rules, check with the college you are considering or its athletic association. Each association distributes a recruiting guide for student-athletes, which is important for you to read.

⚽ Official campus visits are invitational trips for highly recruited student-athletes. The visits may be fully or partially paid for by the college and are closely regulated.

⚽ Although the rules and regulations regarding recruiting can be confusing, they are meant to protect the student-athlete. It is the responsibility of recruits and college representatives to know and abide by the rules.

⚽ Illegal recruiting can cause the student-athlete to lose eligibility to play intercollegiate sports. Knowing a few basic rules can help recruits recognize whether they are being illegally recruited.

Financial aid can often make the difference between being able to attend the college of your choice and having to settle for less. The athletic scholarship itself may pay only a portion of the student-athlete's collegiate expenses, but it is often supplemented with other forms of financial assistance. Chapter 12 tells you about financial aid and how to find out whether you qualify. ⫸

12

Financial Aid:
More than Just Scholarships

"The internet provides a wealth of financial information for free. The federal government, state financial aid programs, college financial aid offices and non-profit organizations have excellent websites that can save you time and give you the information you need to maximize your financial aid resources."

Susan Gutierrez
Director of Financial Aid
Sonoma State University, California

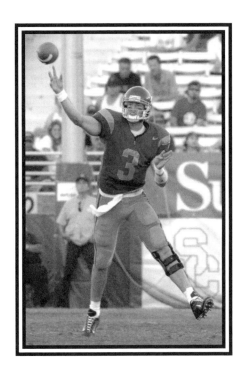

Financial Aid Pays Off

College costs make financial aid, including scholarships, increasingly valuable. In addition to rising college expenses, studies show that state financial aid appropriations per full-time student in higher education continue to decrease nationwide. This loss of funding has caused colleges to cut budgets and created a larger gap between a family's resources and the actual dollars needed to fund the college experience. However, do not let these high costs discourage you from applying to the school of your choice. Scholarships, grants, subsidized loans and other forms of financial aid offer a solution.

What Is Financial Aid?

Over half of the students now in U.S. colleges and universities receive some kind of financial aid. Financial aid is monetary assistance available to students with financial need that is used to pay for part or all of their education. Many types of aid are available to all students who qualify because of financial "need," defined as the difference between your educational expenses—including tuition, fees, room and board, books and supplies and miscellaneous expenses—and the amount you and your family can afford to pay.

Fill out financial aid forms

Other kinds of financial aid in the form of scholarships or educational loans are available to students who do not have financial need according to this definition. Sources of financial aid include the colleges themselves, federal and state governments, private organizations, businesses and lending institutions. Four basic categories of financial aid are available:

- Scholarships
- Grants
- Educational loans
- Work-study programs

Scholarships and Grants

Scholarships = free money!

Scholarships are awards based on academic standing or other achievements. The student's financial need usually is not considered, depending on the source and conditions of the scholarship. So generally speaking, the award is not based on financial necessity. One of the reasons scholarships are so valuable is that they don't have to be repaid. Athletic scholarships, which are based on talent and promise, fall into this category. They are offered by college athletic departments to prospective athletes as an incentive to play for that college or university and are a primary recruiting tool in attracting the best players.

Grants, like scholarships, are not paid back. Grants are awards typically based on financial need, although academic achievement or other factors may be considered. Many federal and state programs award grants, as well as other types of aid.

Scholarships and grants are free money! They are the most desirable of the financial aid options since they do not have to be repaid nor are they time-intensive like a job. Scholarships can run the gamut from small, one-time awards to scholarships worth thousands of dollars, renewable on a yearly basis. Athletic scholarships, like other scholarships, range from full scholarships that pay the costs of tuition and fees, room and board and required books to partial scholarships that pay a portion of college expenses. Mike G., a lacrosse player at an east coast college, receives a scholarship that pays for his tuition and books. "It ends up covering just about half of my expenses," he says. For more on athletic scholarships see Chapter 3.

Athletic scholarships are often combined, or packaged, with other sources of financial aid. Financial aid packages are designed to combine aid based on financial need with other awards. Combinations may include a sports scholarship, state and/or federal government grant, a scholarship from the college and a scholarship from your hometown, along with a federal loan and a work-study award. Using available resources to provide each student the best possible package of aid is one of the major responsibilities of college financial aid offices.

Jennifer P., from Kingwood, Texas, who remembers considering her college and soccer program choices, says, "I spoke with a number of coaches who said they had scholarship monies available, but their schools did not offer the combination of athletics and academics I was looking for. The school I chose put together a financial aid package that consisted of several academic scholarships, grants, work-study and loans."

Educational Loans

Loans must be repaid

Loans are frequently a necessary part of the financial aid package. In fact, most students graduate owing money. Educational loans are similar to other kinds of loans but educational loans from the federal government and some colleges offer attractive terms that you would never get from an ordinary consumer loan. Even so, it's important to remember that educational loans are borrowed funds that must be paid back.

Susan Gutierrez, Director of Financial Aid at Sonoma State University, California, says families have become increasingly savvy about both the costs and benefits of educational loans. "Many students are eligible for subsidized federal loans, which means the cost of interest is paid by the government during the time the student is in school and for a certain period before repayment begins.

"It's always important to understand the terms of an educational loan, including whether the interest will be subsidized or unsubsidized and what your estimated monthly payments will be once you are finished with school."

The trend in financial aid overall is towards more loans and fewer scholarships. "However," says Gutierrez, "investing in your future in this way can really pay off as long as you keep your total borrowing in line with your earning potential."

Work-Study

Work-study is a part-time job program, often right on campus, that enables students to earn money for college expenses by working while they are going to school. College work-study can be an essential part of the financial aid package. The program provides a part-time job on campus or with a non-profit organization off campus for which the student gets paid an hourly wage for a set amount of time, usually up to 20 hours per week. Eligibility for a work-study award is based on financial need. For athletes, however, working part time can be grueling on top of already heavy athletic and academic schedules.

Tom R., from North Carolina, received a partial scholarship that paid for tuition and books. On top of that, he borrowed $2,000 a year through the educational loan program. "I still couldn't quite make it, though," says the former first baseman. "So, as part of my work-study award, I worked in the baseball office for two hours a day, five days a week, during my first three years in college." Although the job took one more chunk of time out of an already busy schedule, Tom says it offered him benefits on top of the money it paid by teaching him to manage his time and helping him prepare for a career.

Work-study is not the only form of student employment. Working one's way through college has always been a viable option, and colleges and universities need student employees to help keep operations running smoothly. Working on campus is convenient and saves valuable time traveling to and from a job off campus. Additionally, most campus employers work around students' class schedules. Criteria for student employment differ from school to school. Some campus employers base their criteria on need while others hire candidates who simply apply and qualify for a job.

A sample one-year financial aid package that includes a sports scholarship for a student-athlete at a private university is shown in Table 9.

TABLE 9:
SAMPLE FINANCIAL AID BREAKDOWN

Analysis of Financial Need

Expenses		Resources	
Tuition	$20,000		
Room & Board/Living Expense	6,000		
Books	1,200	Parent Contribution	$5,400
Personal	1,400	Student Contribution, Income	900
Travel	75	Student Contribution, Assets	105
Total Expenses	$28,675	Total Resources	$6,405

Your Financial Need (Expenses less Resources) = $22,270

Sample Financial Aid Package

California Grant A	$9,036
Athletic Scholarship	8,734
Subsidized Educational Loan	2,500
Academic Year Job Eligibility (work-study)	2,000
Total Offer	$22,270

Also, you may find your financial aid offer includes an unsubsidized student or parent educational loan that can be used to finance the student and/or parent contributions.

Other Sources of Financial Aid

Locating other sources of scholarships or ways to save important tuition dollars and reduce your overall college costs is up to you. If you have any questions about how to access these opportunities, contact your guidance counselor or look at one of the various guides for financial aid.

Out-of-state tuition waivers

Because most state-supported colleges charge out-of-state residents extra tuition, another way colleges provide aid to a recruited athlete is through a *tuition fee waiver*. They forgo the extra tuition charge, saving the student as much as several thousand dollars, depending on the school. Ask the college coach about this option if you think it might apply to you.

Private scholarships

Look for scholarships close to home

Consider community organizations and service clubs, employers and professional, career and trade associations for possible sources for scholarships. Talk to your parents about groups they belong to that offer scholarships to members, and check with your counselor regularly to keep up to date on scholarship opportunities. Consult guides to college scholarships and financial aid from your school or public library or on the internet. Scholarship search services also offer assistance, for a fee. See Resources list on page 164.

"Internet resources for free scholarship searches have exploded in the last few years. There are some fantastic free tools. But, be wary of any service that charges a fee in return for a guaranteed amount of financial aid. Also, be careful about the privacy practices of these services. You want to know whether your personal information will be sold by the service and make an informed choice about whether or not you are okay with that," says Financial Aid Director Susan Gutierrez.

Reduction of school time

High school students can take the College Board's Advanced Placement (AP) exams and receive college *credit* in specialized subjects in which they have proven proficiency. By not having to take courses in these subjects when they get to college, they can save the cost of up to one year of study. Some students also take community college classes during their high school career to help them get some of their general education classes out of the way.

The military

Some very generous scholarships and student aid programs are available to those willing to serve in the U.S. military for a specified period of time after graduation. ROTC (Reserve Officers Training Corps) scholarships are federally funded programs administered by the United States Armed Services. Additionally, military academies offer athletic programs and full payment of fees to qualified candidates. Appointment by a U.S. congressperson is usually necessary. Ask your counselor for more information about military scholarship programs or contact an armed forces recruiting office.

Applying for Financial Aid

It is the job of financial aid counselors to put together the award packages, but first, you must supply them with information about you and your family's financial situation. When you apply to a college, you will be asked whether you want to request financial aid materials. University of Iowa's Mark Warner advises students to always say 'yes' and to inquire about any financial aid they might qualify for. "Every applicant should apply for everything at the beginning."

The required application for all federal aid and most need-based state and institutional aid is the *Free Application for Federal Student Aid (FAFSA)*. You may file the application electronically on the FAFSA website at www.fafsa.ed.gov or get forms from any high school counseling office or college financial aid office. Colleges often require forms in addition to the FAFSA.

Your high school counselor can help answer general financial aid questions when you begin to look for colleges. As you narrow your college search, contact the financial aid office at the college or colleges you are considering for specific information. Each school is different, even colleges in the same state. Make sure you are familiar with the financial aid rules and deadlines for the individual schools.

Other Ways to Locate Financial Assistance for College

Research financial aid options

High school counseling offices or career centers usually have books and guides to inform you about financial aid in general and scholarships in particular. Or, if there is a college nearby, you can probably gain permission to use its facilities to do your research. Most counseling and career centers have financial aid and scholarship search software that is available for student use, or you can research financial aid websites. Another place to find resource materials is your local public library. Reference librarians are trained to help patrons look for information. They can be a tremendous resource if you ask for their assistance. See Resources list on pages 164 and 165 for collegiate financial aid guides and internet websites.

There are also commercial scholarship and financial aid search services available. Students provide information about themselves, pay a fee and get back a computerized list of scholarships and other forms of financial aid for which they might qualify, along with contact information. Some of these businesses are better than others. Many financial aid experts point out that research which students can do themselves costs them nothing more than time.

Some of these businesses offer additional assistance, such as college and financial aid consulting. If you engage one of these businesses, you will want to find out in advance the following:

- what fees they charge
- what services they provide
- whether they have experience with the special needs of student-athletes
- several names of student-athletes they have worked with (and their e-mail addresses and phone numbers) so you can contact them and learn about their level of satisfaction with the consulting service

Of course, if you know people who have used this kind of business, you can ask whether they were happy with it. One more person who might be able to refer you is your high school counselor.

The College Financial Aid Office

Make friends with the financial aid office

The college financial aid office can be very helpful if you have questions when filling out your forms. When you call the office for information, ask to speak with a financial aid counselor (or the director of financial aid, if it is a fairly small school). If you find the counselor easy to talk to, ask for that person's name and write it down. The next time you call, ask to speak to the same counselor. That way you start developing a rapport that will prove extremely helpful down the road. Making a friend in the financial aid office can save you hours of time and frustration over the span of your college years. Also look on the college website for "frequently asked questions" about financial aid and filling out forms.

Tips for Applying for Financial Aid

Beware of Deadlines

As you fill out applications to colleges and apply for financial aid, pay attention to deadlines. There are important dates by which time you must do something: turn in an application, respond to a request for information or pay a fee. Colleges and other financial aid agencies are very strict about deadlines. A deadline missed is often a lost opportunity and can make the difference between being considered for a scholarship or losing out entirely. Missing a deadline can mean not being able to attend your first choice of school, or you might end up paying thousands of dollars more for your education than you would have had you met the deadline.

As suggested in Chapter 6, use a calendar to help you keep track of important dates. Each time you find out about a financial aid deadline, write it down on your calendar. Write important deadlines (such as the dates to turn in college applications, fees, etc.) in big print and red ink, and highlight them! We can't stress enough the importance of meeting deadlines.

Allow Enough Time

Start early!

The forms you and your parents are required to fill out for financial aid, in addition to application forms, may seem endless. You might be tempted to put them off until shortly before they are due...but don't! Many require information that may not be at your fingertips but rather needs to be collected or that is dependent on your doing other things first. For instance, both you and your parents may be required to submit figures from your federal income tax statements. Because most financial aid forms are due early in the year, many people run into problems because their previous year's taxes have not yet been computed. Although most institutions allow you to estimate, it is much easier to work from a completed tax return, and institutions often require that you confirm your estimates after filing the tax return.

It is estimated that over 80 percent of students who file for financial aid through

FAFSA do so online. Students can get a PIN number so they and their parents can also sign their online application, which saves time. But, it takes a week or two to get your PIN number after you apply, so do this early.

Before You Send It Off

Before you even consider mailing (or sending online) your FAFSA and any other required financial aid applications, recheck all your figures and be sure you and your parents have signed in the appropriate places. If you are required to send any documentation or other enclosures, make sure all are included.

- Type or write your name and social security number on each sheet of paper you send.
- Make copies of everything you send. Never mail an application that has taken you so long to complete without making copies first. Keep the copy of the application and originals of your other materials.
- If mailing, package your information in a 9 x 11-inch or larger manila envelope and address it correctly with your return address on the envelope.
- Mail the original application to the financial aid office along with copies of all materials.
- The FAFSA is mailed separately in the envelope enclosed in the application packet, while any other required college forms are mailed directly to the college.
- Mail your financial aid forms from the post office so that you can fill out a Certificate of Mailing when you purchase the correct postage. The Certificate of Mailing is inexpensive and is your receipt, showing the date you mailed the envelope. Having this receipt can be extremely important in case the envelope gets lost or fails to arrive by the financial aid deadline.
- Keep all your financial aid copies, along with corroborating information and the Certificate of Mailing, together for easy reference in the file folders for the individual colleges to which you apply.
- Pat yourself on the back for a job well done!

Summary

- The increasing cost of college, together with reduced funding for higher education, makes financial aid more necessary than ever.

- Financial aid packages may consist of several forms of assistance, including scholarships, grants, educational loans and work study.

- Full athletic scholarships are awarded mostly to truly outstanding athletes in major sports, while partial scholarships are given to the majority of student-athletes.

- Athletic scholarships do not have to be repaid and can often be supplemented with other forms of financial aid for students who qualify.

- It is your responsibility to investigate the availability of financial aid by researching opportunities at your high school counseling office or public library and contacting both the coach of your sport and the financial aid office at the colleges in which you are interested.

The number of women in collegiate athletics is increasing as new sports for women are added and more money is available for women's athletic programs. The next chapter tells how to find and take advantage of golden opportunities in women's collegiate sports programs.

13

Golden Opportunities for Female Athletes

"The growth of opportunity for women in sports has been phenomenal. In one generation, we have gone from young girls hoping that there **is** *a team to young girls hoping they can* **make** *the team."*

Mary Jo Kane
Director, Tucker Center for Research on Girls & Women in Sports
University of Minnesota

Intercollegiate Sports Offer Opportunities for Women

Title IX = gender equity

Intercollegiate athletics has made it possible for today's young women to continue to play their sport at the college level and help pay for their education at the same time. But the opportunities for female student-athletes were negligible before passage of *Title IX*, the federal legislation that mandated *gender equity* in education and sports. Your mothers and grandmothers had limited chances to play sports; furthermore, girls who played kickball or baseball in the streets with the neighbor boys were mockingly called "tomboys."

Title IX

Congress passed legislation in 1972 calling for equal opportunity in educational institutions that receive any federal funds. Among other things, this groundbreaking legislation prohibits sex discrimination in sports. Since Title IX was enacted, the world of girls' and women's athletics has virtually exploded with opportunity. In brief, Title IX states:

> No person in the United States shall, on the basis of sex, be excluded from participation in, be denied the benefits of, or be subjected to discrimination under any educational program or activity receiving Federal financial assistance.

As a result of the enactment of Title IX, the number of girls participating in high school and college sports multiplied. In 1971, there were only 294,015 girls participating in high school sports. During the next year that number more than doubled. Similar gains occurred in intercollegiate sports, and athletic scholarships, which had been virtually non-existent for women, were added.

Although more opportunities were rapidly created at the onset of Title IX, momentum slowed because some colleges were not adhering to the spirit of the legislation and because of lack of enforcement. Finally, with the passage of the Civil Rights Restoration Act in March, 1988, Title IX's institution-wide protection against discrimination was reaffirmed. Court decisions in virtually all cases since that time have upheld the provisions of Title IX, and colleges and universities today continue to move towards gender equity.

Clearly, Title IX has created golden opportunities for female student-athletes, with 2.9 million young women participating at the high school level and nearly 167,000 playing collegiate sports in the 2005-06 school year.

"Title IX fundamentally changed the landscape, because without it, we [females] wouldn't be where we are," says Mary Jo Kane, director of the Tucker Center for Research on Girls & Women in Sports, University of Minnesota. "For the first time in history we have a critical mass of girls and women who play sports. You have young girls who grow up with a sense of entitlement towards sports. It would never occur to them that an opportunity *wouldn't* be available to them."

There was clearly not that sense of entitlement for Kane, who played football, basketball and baseball with her childhood friends in central Illinois during the 1960s but had no opportunity to play organized sports at her high school. She became a cheerleader, as did many other sports-minded young women of those times. It was the closest they could get to the game.

Benefits of Sports

Today, unlike in the days before Title IX and gender equity, a woman's well-defined calf and firm triceps are considered attractive as well as feminine. In many families, young girls play catch with their fathers and brothers, while their moms are off playing softball or running a 10K race. For females of all ages who are physically active and play sports, the rewards are great.

Many girls say that what they like about sports is having fun, making friends, keeping busy and being in shape. Fortunately for them, research compiled by the Women's Sports Foundation indicates that participation in sports has tremendous benefits for girls. Females who participate in sports are healthier, happier, less likely to participate in risk-taking behavior and more likely to get an education.

As little girls grow into women who are encouraged to be physically active, their self-confidence and skills grow and they find increased opportunities to use their athletic talent…before, during and after college.

Sports Benefits for Females

Females of all ages who participate in sports:

- Have higher levels of self-esteem than nonathletes
- Suffer less depression than nonathletes
- Develop a more positive body image than nonathletes
- Decrease their risk of obesity
- Lower their risk of breast cancer
- Lower their risk of osteoporosis and heart disease

Girls who participate in sports are:

- 3 times more likely to graduate from high school
- 80% less likely to have an unwanted pregnancy
- 92% less likely to use drugs

College females who participate in sports:

- Have access to athletic scholarships to help pay their educations
- Are more likely to graduate at a significantly higher rate than the overall female student population

Sports for Her, A Reference Guide for Teenage Girls, by Penny Hastings, Greenwood Press, 1999.

Emerging Sports for Women

Title IX legislation brought about funding for current women's programs and the promotion of women's teams from club to varsity or collegiate status. New sports, called *emerging sports,* were also added to college athletic programs to provide more women the opportunity to play a greater number of intercollegiate sports. Emerging sports are vital to the growth of women's intercollegiate athletics because, by their designation, they become part of the school's athletic department and so are financially supported like other intercollegiate sports rather than funded by cupcake sales and car washes, as are club teams.

Additionally, participants of emerging sports are eligible for sports scholarship awards. Earlier emerging sports, such as ice hockey and rowing, have gained enough teams now to become full-fledged intercollegiate sports.

Young women with athletic backgrounds can sometimes take advantage of emerging sports even though they may have little or no proficiency in that new sport. Oftentimes an emerging college sport has few high school programs to draw from so the coaches recruit athletes in other sports for their fledgling programs. Jane LaRivierie, women's rowing coach, Washington State University, says her program now has more experienced high school and club athletes to recruit than it did ten years ago, when women's rowing was an early emerging sport. However, she suggests this to skilled athletes who are interested in rowing: "For girls who haven't rowed before, send us videos of the sports you play so we can see how you look as an athlete."

The NCAA has assigned emerging-sports status to the following sports: archery, badminton, bowling, equestrian, rugby, squash, synchronized swimming and team handball.

Because equestrian is relatively new at the intercollegiate level, many young horsewomen are unaware of its existence. Pamela Bruemmer, equestrian coach at New Mexico State University, says, "Equestrian is not as mainstream as the major sports like basketball and soccer. A lot of girls don't know about their college opportunities."

For the most part, equestrian is not a high school sport, so coaches are limited to looking elsewhere for athletes. "We try to recruit girls who have riding experience at the regional, state and national levels. Sometimes, though, we can't find enough experienced riders, so we'll take girls who are interested in learning and have shown they are hard working in other sports," says Bruemmer.

The NCAA allows 15 equestrian scholarships for each Division I and II school. "We can divide up the scholarships," says Bruemmer. "That allows us to help more athletes."

Women are Still Underrepresented

Despite increased opportunities in collegiate sports for women, the number of men competing at the college level is greater than that of women, even though females make up more than half of the college student bodies. (In 2005 there were 222,838 men compared to 166,728 women competing in intercollegiate sports.)

It's not 50 - 50!

According to the Women's Sports Foundation in its *2006 State of Women's Sports Report*, females comprise 57 percent of the college student population. Yet, women's sports get only 33 percent of the college athletic recruiting budget. Donna Lopiano, executive director of the Women's Sports Foundation, says, "$1.1 billion is awarded each year in athletic scholarships, but females receive only 43 percent."

"Even though there has been phenomenal growth for female athletes over the last decade, are the opportunities for women equal to men? The answer is no," states Mary Jo Kane, director, Tucker Center for Research on Girls & Women in Sports, University of Minnesota.

Women Have To Try Harder!

Although opportunities have steadily increased, women still have to try harder than men to get recruited. Because two-thirds of college recruiting budgets is allotted to men's sports, many female student-athletes go unnoticed. That means it is even more important for girls to market their talents and bring themselves to the attention of college coaches.

Lopiano says, "There's an imbalance. The [annual] recruiting budgets for women's sports are $72,000 less than for men's. Additionally, male athletes get $137 million dollars more in athletic scholarships."

Therefore, even if you're a blue-chip player, you can't assume that coaches are going to come to you. And, if you're among the 99 percent of student-athletes who are not superstars, the need to be proactive and start the recruiting process yourself is even greater. While the rush to equalize women's sports gives today's female student-athletes an edge over their predecessors, Kane points out: "It's not a 50/50 proposition. Women are competing for a smaller pool of resources."

Jennifer P., a four-year women's college soccer player, believes her sport helped her get into Stanford, a school with one of the most competitive admissions policies in the nation.

Female athletes need to market themselves!

Jennifer was a blue-chip soccer player in high school. Because she played on state and regional teams, she had the opportunity to be seen by college coaches at high-profile tournaments. However, she says she actively participated in her own recruitment by writing letters to coaches at colleges that interested her. "I didn't want to leave it up to chance. I know of several very talented players who could have easily played for a Division I soccer team but abandoned the idea because they weren't actively recruited." Jennifer received a few scholarship offers and chose Stanford because of its academic reputation.

We have stressed in this book that you don't have to be a superstar to win an athletic scholarship. But for women, Jennifer's story shows that even very outstanding female athletes need to help their cause by marketing themselves. Other players with less visibility have to put forth more effort to get recognized.

Although the process for winning a sports scholarship is basically the same as for men, women must draw attention to their talents even more vigorously. They must start the recruiting process early by making contact with college coaches, rather than waiting to be contacted.

Being proactive can make the difference between being noticed or not. Shellie Onstead, field hockey coach, University of California, says, "I spend most of my evaluation time looking at players who have already shown an interest in my program. Athletes who fail to contact me and wait to be noticed may be overlooked at an event because I am focusing on other athletes."

Don't leave recruiting to chance!

Kim Sutton, women's soccer coach, CSU Chico, California, concurs: "At club tournaments every one of the college coaches is looking at those kids who contacted them. If I don't know about you, I will probably not notice you unless you have a purple mohawk!"

After initial contact, continue to be proactive by reminding coaches at colleges that interest you of new accomplishments and awards, updated schedules and your continuing interest in the school. By being proactive and persistent, your chances of grabbing the attention of college coaches and causing them to recruit you increase dramatically.

More Opportunities for Female Athletes after College

Few women go on to play professional sports, mainly because opportunities are limited. Tennis, golf, basketball, volleyball, football (tackle football, not soccer), fast-pitch baseball, track and field and bowling are some of the sports that either pay team members a salary, as in the Women's National Basketball Association (WNBA), or award prize money, as in pro golf and tennis.

Sports after college

In the U.S. and worldwide, the number of women who participate in pro sports is small, but some organizations, such as the WNBA, have survived and even flourished. The league celebrated its 10th anniversary in 2006, making it the longest running American-based women's professional league in history. Women athletes such as Mia Hamm (soccer), Lisa Leslie (basketball), Danicka Patrick (car racing), Annika Sorenstam (golf) and Serena and Venus Williams (tennis) have become household names.

But the biggest benefit for women who play sports as youngsters and during college is that they are more likely than their nonathletic peers to remain active in their adult lives. They often continue to play their sport in adult recreational leagues or take up new sports. Some compete well into their senior years. Jan Condon, a California resident and long-time runner, decided to learn the high jump. She became an All-American Masters' high-jumper during her 50's. Now in her mid-60's, she still competes in Masters' track and field events.

Besides participation, many women stay involved with athletics through career choices. Women work in sports medicine, management, marketing and manufacturing for sports-related businesses, and many other sports-career areas. They also often encourage younger sisters and daughters to enter these and other occupations that used to be overwhelmingly dominated by men. According to the Women's Sports Foundation, there are over six million jobs in sport-related careers. Julie Foudy, former USA Women's World Cup soccer team captain and a founding member of the Women's Professional Soccer League (2000-2003), is now a television sports commentator and political policy consultant.

Employers value female athletes

Other opportunities in non-sports-related careers are available to women athletes, who are often perceived to be strong candidates for employment because of the skills they mastered participating in sports. Lessons learned on the playing field transfer superbly to the work place. Donna Lopiano, executive director of the Women's Sports Foundation, believes American business is based on the sports model. "Sports is one of the most socio-cultural learning environments in our society," she says.

Many employers say that they view prospective employees with an athletic background as highly desirable in the work place, especially those who have played at the college level. According to a study by the University of Virginia, 80 percent of women identified as key leaders in Fortune 500 companies participated in sports during their youth. Besides leadership, other highly prized traits common to successful student-athletes include these:

- self-confidence
- high energy
- physical strength and agility
- ability to work in a team setting
- assertiveness
- competitiveness
- persistence
- ability to focus
- high motivation

For females the benefits of sports participation often begins with backyard foot races, water balloon tossing and tetherball. At six years and younger, they start playing t-ball and soccer along with bike riding and swimming. They continue on with high school volleyball and softball and into collegiate sports such as rowing, track and field, soccer, water polo and tennis. Sports scholarships and careers provide financial rewards, while adult participation, often into the senior years, offers fitness and fun.

Summary

⚽   Today women and girls participate in competitive sports in record numbers as a result of federal legislation (Title IX).

⚽   Beginning in 1972, Title IX mandated that gender equity be brought into balance at collegiate institutions.

⚽   Today a woman's athletic talent can pay her way through college.

⚽   For women to take advantage of the golden opportunities in college athletics, they have to attract the attention of college coaches by marketing themselves.

⚽   The overall benefits of sports for women carry over into the work place and throughout a lifetime.

Chapter 14 tells you how to put together the rewards for all your hard work: your acceptance into the college of your choice and hopefully, an athletic scholarship. You will get hints to help you get ready for your college experience and 25 tips for success from college student-athletes who have already gone through the exciting, often bewildering, first few weeks of college life and intercollegiate sports. ⏩

14

Making It All Work

You're on Your Way

Making the Decision

Most athletes are happy with their college choice

By now you may have made your college selection, and after being offered one (or more) athletic scholarships, signed your letter of intent. Or perhaps, despite your effort, you were not offered a scholarship. Don't be discouraged. There are many success stories of student-athletes who were not recruited by a college program out of high school but who enrolled at the college, tried out and made the team, eventually receiving an athletic scholarship. Additionally, because intercollegiate sports are only a small part of athletic opportunities available at most colleges and universities, you can still participate in your sport at the club or intramural level wherever you go to college.

Perhaps you are still in the negotiating stage or trying to make the tough decision between several schools. If so, we wish you good luck! Perhaps it will help you to know that most college students are happy with their choice of schools, even when they agonized over the decision and weren't sure they had finally selected the right one.

Also keep in mind that choosing a college is not a forever choice. If, for some reason, you find yourself unhappy or dissatisfied after the first year you can transfer to another institution or take a break while you decide on your options. However, it is best to give yourself an entire school year to make the adjustment and decide if you want to continue.

You should know that transferring creates unique problems if you are a student-athlete. To transfer schools as a scholarship student-athlete is even harder. The coach at the new school must want you and a scholarship spot must be available, or you might still join the team as a non-scholarship student-athlete. It is also possible you will have to sit out a year without being able to compete.

Check very carefully with the college athletic directors involved, the compliance officers at each school and athletic associations to which each college belongs for the correct procedures to follow when you are considering transferring to another four-year institution or to a community college.

Hopefully, like the majority of intercollegiate student-athletes, you will be satisfied with your college and athletic program choice. So now that you've made the decision, can you breathe a sigh of relief? Yes! Can you kick back, forget your studies and slack off on your skill building and athletic training? NO!

Staying Motivated

Scholastically, you have passed only one hurdle—that of getting accepted to the college. Read the fine print on your acceptance letter. It says you have been conditionally accepted, pending final grades and proof of high school graduation. That means that your senior year's grades count and that your admission can be rescinded if you fail to maintain the academic standards that impressed the college coaches and admissions officials.

Sports-wise, it is definitely NOT the time to kick back. Whether you've signed a letter of intent or plan to *walk on* (try out) after you get to college, you must arrive in peak condition, with your skills honed razor-sharp. That means competing at the highest level possible in your senior year and during the following summer. It means pushing yourself towards an ever-higher level of excellence.

"Don't be satisfied dominating high school or club competition. Push yourself to be better than the players you are striving to compete against at the next level," advises Craig F., former Division I volleyball player.

In some ways, the pressure will be less after you are accepted because you won't have to wonder whether scouts are watching you and worry about impressing college coaches or recruiters. But in other ways, the pressure is even greater, with your coaches and teammates knowing that you are going on to compete at the collegiate level and perhaps expecting even more from you.

Mainly, you need to stay motivated and focused for your own good. The more you apply yourself both academically and athletically, the better you will do when you move from your familiar high school environment to the rigorous demands of college.

Russ Peterich, high school golf coach, declares, "Once you get a scholarship and make the team, your athletic life is just beginning. You need to prepare yourself for a whole new game."

Don't kick back; play hard!

You Have What It Takes

While it can be difficult to combat "senioritis," you, more than most students, can successfully keep your balance and focus on your goals. Why? Because you have already proved you have the time management skills and determination to excel in two different and often conflicting areas—academics and athletics. You are also bright enough to know that college, at all levels, will undoubtedly be more difficult than anything you have experienced up to this time.

So far you have excelled; you have been one of the top competitors on your high school or club team. Once you get to college, though, you will meet other student-athletes who are just as talented or even more so than you. Whether you can compete in that more rarefied environment depends on your maturity, motivation, skill development and level of fitness.

Keeping Your Body And Mind Fit

Get in Shape; Stay in Shape

In the months following the completion of your senior high school sports season, you may still be competing on a club team or playing another sport, which will help you keep in shape. However, following a fall or winter sport, there may not be a club team or other group you can join. In that case, to assure that your skills don't get rusty and you stay physically fit, plan a daily workout schedule—join a gym, run or swim laps, train with weights. You know best what kinds of activities you need to do in order to play your sport. You might also ask your high school or club coach to help you plan a workout schedule.

Additionally, your college coach may send you a training schedule. Sam Koch, men's soccer coach at University of Massachusetts makes this recommendation: "Adhere to your training instructions strictly. Coaches make these schedules for a reason. We know what it takes to get you into shape to play at the college level. If you are involved in other training, however, let the coach know so he or she can adjust your workout."

Karen Stanley, women's soccer coach at Santa Rosa Junior College in California, suggests: "During the summer before starting a four-year college, take a sports- or weight-training class at your nearest community college, or talk to the two-year college coach in your sport about a training schedule."

Don't give in to senioritis!

Many student-athletes compete in summer leagues following high school. Baseball players in some areas play Connie Mack or American Legion ball. Others play in a rookie league, where they compete with other college-bound or current college players. This gives them the chance to "play up" a notch, experience collegiate-style competition and gain additional practice and playing time.

Other sports, too, usually have teams or competitive events that continue long past the high school playing season. You may participate on these teams as long as your amateur status is not compromised.

NCAA and other athletic associations have strict criteria for defining what constitutes amateur and professional status. Your college coach should make you aware of the criteria. Moreover, you can call the athletic association to which your college belongs to get a written statement of policy.

NCAA prospects and recruits are required to complete a questionnaire about their athletic history as it relates to contracts, salaries and other benefits that could affect their amateur status. Beginning with student-athletes planning to enter college starting in the fall of 2007, this questionnaire will be included in the Initial Eligibility Clearinghouse registration process.

Being awarded an athletic scholarship does not definitely mean you have made the first team. You may have to earn your place in *preseason* tryouts along with the other rookies, not to mention the walk-ons, who have extra incentive to impress the coach and win a place on the team and possibly even a scholarship.

Student-athletes whom we interviewed overwhelmingly reported that one of the hardest adjustments they had to make was in the level of physical endurance and fitness they were expected to meet to perform at the college level.

Work out over the summer

Chris P., former Stanford University soccer player, states, "Every athlete should be on a weight-training program. The hard transition is the physical one. If you can get a head start and begin adding muscle before you get to college, it will make a big difference."

Former Division I volleyball player, Mike L., advises, "Train hard the last three or four months (at least) before you begin college athletics. For me, the level of training was much higher in college than in high school. Remember, you are going to be competing against players who have played at the collegiate level for one to four years before you arrived. You need to get yourself prepared, both physically and mentally, in order to beat out a more mature athlete for a position or place on the team."

Karen A., former Division I volleyball player, says, "Since I had such high expectations of college volleyball, I worked out the summer before more than ever. I came into preseason in the best shape I'd ever been in. It really helped."

"The level of fitness was a step higher once I got to the college level. It was OK, but let me tell you, it sure was easy to lose my fitness level in college. It was so much easier to stay in shape in high school; it just came naturally. In college I had to work to stay in shape. The level was that much higher," remembers Chris H., former goal-keeper, Division I soccer.

It's Never Too Early to Start Getting Ready

★

Make a successful leap into college!

As an intercollegiate athlete, you will probably have to report to college earlier than the general student body. If yours is a fall sport, you may have to be there a month or more before school starts, which means you will have a short summer. On top of all that, you will want to spend time with your friends and family, plus get clothes and necessities for furnishing your dorm room or apartment. The summer after you graduate from high school goes by in a flash.

Learning to balance your priorities is of paramount importance once you enter college. The academic demands alone take some adjustment. When you add the commitment of an intercollegiate sport, you must become a master of time management to succeed. Mike L., former Division I volleyball player, makes this suggestion: "Research what your time commitment will be and start getting into that mind frame before you get to college."

Current or former collegiate student-athletes who have gone through it before you can be a huge help as you prepare to make the leap from high school to college sports.

Making a Successful Transition to College Sports

- Plan a daily workout schedule and stick to it.
- Develop a weight-training program.
- Continue to play your sport.
- Compete at the highest level possible.
- Learn as much as you can about your new team.
- Talk to future teammates about the level of play you can expect.
- Ask for suggestions about how you can prepare yourself.
- Follow the workout schedule set by your college coach.
- Ask advice from college students about college life in general.
- Enjoy your family and high school friends; before you know it, summer will be over.

Advice from College Student-Athletes

Current and former college student-athletes, men and women—in different sports and all three athletic divisions—remember how overwhelmed they felt when they first entered college. Here they reveal their memories and offer suggestions to the rookies—student-athletes like you.

"You have to be extremely disciplined as far as allotting enough time for studies, sleep, socializing and sports. Prioritize well and listen to your body; don't overextend yourself. It's very easy to get carried away in the social scene with new friends, new activities. A lot of freshmen athletes get sick or injured simply because they're overly tired."

"It's important to come into college ready to learn…not as if you already know it all."

"Be patient! Many college athletes want to come in and start or contribute in a big way right away. I know I did. However, four years is a long time. It's more of a marathon than a sprint. It can be an emotional roller coaster if you expect too much right away. It's better to focus on improving over the course of a year than it is to worry about who's starting next week."

"Prepare to spend more time involved with your sport than most other students do who work at a part-time job."

"Get into the best shape of your life! It will help you to avoid injuries early in training camp and will earn you the respect of your teammates and coach as they see that you are very committed to furthering the goals of the team."

"Be prepared to schedule your time very efficiently. You'll be in classes all morning, practice all afternoon, then possibly working or studying during the evening."

"Try and find activities outside of your sport. Join a fraternity or sorority, be active in your dorm, and join different student groups—it's important to have outlets outside of your sport that are fun."

"Realize that an intercollegiate sport is more like a job than a 'just for fun' activity. It's more intense because a coach's job relies, in part, upon how well the team does. The coach passes that intensity on to the team."

"Approach your sport as you would a job, with the same intensity and time commitment."

"Be prepared for not being the star, but only one out of many, many others."

"Remember that in most instances the success of not only the coaching staff but of the entire institution is often measured by the success of its athletic program. You will be judged according to these standards."

"You may not be treated as a professional, but if you want to succeed, you had better act like one!"

"At the high school level, most motivation comes from the coach keeping things together. Once you get to college, you have to motivate yourself."

"Don't go to college with the idea of putting all of your efforts into sports, or your college education won't be the awesome experience that it should be."

"Get yourself in great shape before arriving at school and be ready to go hard. Prepare yourself to compete for a spot [on the team] and continue to compete all year for that spot. If you play in a top program, starting spots are never safe."

"You are expected to show commitment and intensity. Some players have that intensity in high school, but in college almost everyone has it. If you don't put 100 percent into the team, you will hear about it from your teammates."

"Time management is the key to success for the college student-athlete. Being able to get the most out of your college experience and balancing the three major areas—academic, athletic and social—without letting any one of these elements suffer at the hands of another is a challenge."

"Be prepared for long practices and road trips and staying up late to study."

"Don't go to college for the sport alone. You may get hurt and be unable to participate for a year or for the remainder of your college career."

"Stay in shape over the summer before college starts. College training is hard enough when you're in shape; no need to kill yourself just to get in shape."

"There are some negative aspects of playing a collegiate sport. It not only cuts into study time but also severely restricts the amount of time you can spend on other interests while at college. However, if you choose wisely, you can experience most of what you want to while at school."

"Don't forget: in order to play ball, you have to stay in school. Find a study schedule that fits your individual needs and style. That could mean classes in the morning, study before practice, then practice; or it could mean lots of late nights in order to get your work done."

"Juggling college classes with sports and being away from home for the first time was a revelation. It would have been hard enough without the sports."

"Everyone needs a break sometimes. Make sure you find time away from your sport, even during the season. It will keep you sane!"

"Have fun! If it's not fun for you, there's no sense in continuing."

Summary

- The skills you have developed getting into college and trying to win a sports scholarship will help you through your lifetime.

- Most student-athletes are satisfied with their college choice, although alternatives such as transferring to another college or deciding not to continue on with college sports are options open to you.

- An athletic scholarship both rewards you and obligates you to live up to certain requirements.

- Being accepted to college and receiving your athletic scholarship is not an end but a beginning of the next step in your academic and athletic life.

- Use the time before you enter college to increase your level of skill and fitness, both mentally and physically.

- Balancing sports, studies, socializing and sleep may be the biggest challenge you face in college.

- Don't take it all too seriously. HAVE FUN!

Appendix

Sports Resume Worksheet

Personal Information:

Full Name: _____

Address: _____

Phone Number: _____ Cell Phone Number: _____

E-mail Address: _____ Height: _____ Weight: _____

Jersey Number High School: _____ Jersey Number Club: _____

Academic Information:

Grade Point Average (GPA): _____

Class Rank: _____

PSAT Score: _____

SAT Score: _____

ACT Score: _____

Academic Awards and Achievements: _____

_____

_____

Athletic Information:

Sport: _____

Position(s) played: _____

Current Team/Organization: _____

Recent Accomplishments: _____

Athletic Awards:

   Individual: _____

_____

   Team: _____

Other Sports: _____

Other Information:

Leadership Roles: _____

Clubs and Organizations: _____

_____

Community Service: _____

Employment: _____

References:

Name: _____ Relationship: _____

Contact Information: _____

Name: _____ Relationship: _____

Contact Information: _____

Name: _____ Relationship: _____

Contact Information: _____

College Information Worksheet

Name of Institution: _____

Institution Website: _____

Location: _____

Student-body Size: _____

Academic Requirements:

Average GPA: _____

Average SAT: _____

Average ACT: _____

Major Areas of Study: _____

Requested General Information about School: _____

Received Info: _____

Received Application: _____

Number of Recommendations Requested: _____

Notes: _____

_____

_____

Athletic Information:

Sport: _____

Coach's Name: _____

Coach's Address: _____

Coach's E-mail Address: _____

Coach's Phone Number: _____ Coach's Cell Phone Number: _____

Athletic Division: _____

Number of Scholarships Available: _____ Graduation Rate of Athletes in Your Sport: _____

Sent Initial Contact Letter: _____

Sent Sports Resume Kit: _____

Follow-up Calls and E-mails: _____

_____

Scholarship Offer: _____

_____

Notes: _____

_____

_____

Other Information:

Housing Availability: _____

Freshman Roommate: _____

Work-study Availability: _____

APPLICATION DUE DATE: _____

College Rating Sheet

(Rate each institution on a 1–5 scale, with 5 being the highest.)

Factors to Consider	Rating 1-5	Name of College	Name of College	Name of College	Name of College	Name of College
Total						

Materials Tracking Chart

School	Requested General Info.	Received General Info.	Initial Contact Letter Sent	Received Info. from Coach	Sports Resume Package Sent	Follow-up Call/e-mail	Sent Add'l Info. (Videos, DVDs etc.)	Application Due Date	Sent Application

Resources
Books
College Guides—Academic

Barron's Profiles of American Colleges: Descriptions of the Colleges 2007, Barron's Educational Services, Inc., an index of college majors state-by-state, as well as facts, finances and profiles of American colleges. www.impactpublications.com

The College Handbook 2007, College Board Publications. Helpful resource guide to information about colleges and universities. www.store.collegeboard.com

The Complete Book of Colleges, 2007 edition, by the Princeton Review, Random House, Inc. An overall guide to admissions, campus life, financial aid and athletic programs. www.princetonreview.com

The Fiske Guide to Colleges 2007, Sourcebooks, Inc. Includes a section on best buys as well as tips and advice from students. www.fiskeguide.com

The Fiske Guide to Getting into the Right College, 2006, Sourcebooks, Inc. Takes you behind the scenes of the college admissions process. www.fiskeguide.com

The Insider's Guide to the Colleges, 2007, compiled and edited by the staff of The Yale Daily News, St. Martin's Press. A guide written by current students from coast-to-coast who tell what their colleges are really like.

Peterson's Guide to Four-Year Colleges, 2007, Peterson's Guides, Princeton, NJ; detailed resource guide to help students learn about colleges and universities. www.petersons.com

College Guides—Athletic

Blue Book of College Athletics for Senior, Junior & Community Colleges, 2007, by Athletic Publishing Company. (205) 263-4436. www.athleticpubco.com

A Guide for the College-Bound Student, 2007-08, publication of the National Association of Intercollegiate Athletics, which includes basic eligibility regulations, financial assistance policies and recruitment policies of the NAIA. Call (913) 791-0044. www.naia.org

A Guide for College-Bound Student-Athletes and Their Parents, 2006. A helpful guide for the college and athletic program selection process. Prepared by the National Interscholastic Athletic Administrators Association and distributed through the National Federation of State High School Associations. Call (800) 776-3462 to order. For information go to www.niaa.org or call (317) 822-5715.

NCAA Guide for the College-Bound Student-Athlete, 2007-08. An annual guide to recruiting rules and academic requirements; available at high school counseling offices or by contacting the National Collegiate Athletic Association (317) 917-6222. www.ncaa.org

NCAA Guide for the Two-Year College Student-Athlete, 2007-08. An annual publication that explains NCAA rules to student-athletes, parents and two-year college athletics administrators; available at community college counseling offices or by contacting the National Collegiate Athletic Association (NCAA). (317) 917-6222. www.ncaa.org

Peterson's Guide to Sports Scholarships and College Athletic Programs, 2006. Institutions offering athletics by sport, division and gender, with contact information for coaches and admissions. (800) 338-3282. www.petersons.com

College Guides—Scholarships/Financial Aid

Reference Service Press publishes a variety of biennially updated books about financial aid, including the *Directory of Financial Aid for Women, Financial Aid for African Americans, Financial Aid for Asian Americans, Financial Aid for Hispanic Americans, Financial Aid for Native Americans, High School Senior's Guide to Merit and Other No-Need Funding, Money for Christian College Students,* 2006-08; all books by Gail Ann Schlachter and R. David Weber. (916) 939-9626. www.rspfunding.com

Paying for College Without Going Broke, 2007, by the Princeton Review. From calculating financial aid eligibility to benefiting from educational tax breaks and special circumstances for single parents, this book has useful money-saving information to combat the soaring costs of college tuition. www.princetonreview.com

The Scholarship Book: The Complete Guide to Private Scholarships, Grants & Loans for Undergraduates, 12th edition, by The National Scholarship Research Service, Prentice Hall, Inc. For prospective college students and present undergraduates to learn about the over 50,000 scholarship opportunities in the private-sector.

Funding Education Beyond High School: The Guide to Federal Aid, 2007-08. U.S. Department of Education, Federal Aid Information Center, 1 800-4-FED AID (1 800-433-3243). www.studentaid.ed.gov/students/publications

Women's Sports

Playing Fair: A Guide to Title IX, 2003. Aimed toward helping athletes, coaches, parents and others ensure that girls and women receive equal opportunities in high school and college sports. Women's Sports Foundation, (800) 227-3988. www.womenssportsfoundation.org

Making Her Mark, by Ernestine Miller, Contemporary Books, 2002. A women's history of over 50 sports, from the trailblazers to popular athletes today.

Sports for Her: A Reference Guide for Teenage Girls, by Penny Hastings, Greenwood Press, 1999. A guide for girls that explores the most popular sports at the high school level along with other, less familiar sports, and offers practical advice on training techniques, trying out for the team and organizing school teams. (707) 579-3479. penny@winasportsscholarship.com

Athletic Associations

NCAA (National College Athletic Association), P.O. Box 6222, Indianapolis, IN 46206-6222; (317) 917-6222. www.ncaa.org

NAIA (National Association of Intercollegiate Athletics), 6120 South Yale Ave., Suite 1450, Tulsa, Oklahoma 74136; (918) 494-8828. www.naia.org

NJCAA (National Junior College Athletic Association), P.O. Box 7305, Colorado Springs, CO 80933-7305; (719) 590-9788. www.njcaa.org

NCCAA (National Christian College Athletic Association), 302 West Washington St., Greenville, SC 29601, (864) 250-1199. www.thenccaa.org

Groups, Associations

Higher Education Consultants Association (HECA). A national organization for independent educational consultants, educational services and other professionals. www.hecaonline.org

National Association of College Admission Counseling (NACAC), 1631 Prince St., Alexandria, VA 22314; (800) 822-6285. A national organization of secondary-school counselors and independent educational consultants and other professionals. www.nacacnet.org

National Federation of State High School Associations, PO Box 690, Indianapolis, IN 46206, (317) 972-6900. A national organization, consisting of the fifty individual state high school athletic associations, plus the District of Columbia, that coordinates ideas and programs of members for the benefit of young people in high school sports.

Women's Sports Foundation, Eisenhower Park, East Meadow, NY 11554, 1-800-227-3988; a non-profit educational organization to promote, educate and enhance the sports and fitness experience for all girls and women. www.womenssportsfoundation.org

Websites

www.act.org Information on the ACT test and exploring college choices. Tips on test-taking.

www.collegeboard.com College and scholarship search information.

www.collegecoachesonline.com Comprehensive database of current college coaches at NCAA and NAIA institutions.

www.cpec.ca.gov Guide to 512 degree-granting California colleges.

www.ed.gov/finaid The U.S. Department of Education provides more than $78 billion a year, about 60 percent of all student aid, to help millions of students and families pay for postsecondary education. Learn about the various kinds of financial aid, how to apply and more.

www.educationindex.com Overview of colleges and college rankings.

www.finaid.org FinAid: The SmartStudent Guide to Financial Aid.

www.kaptest.com Guide to test prep and college admissions.

www.princetonreview.com/college Provides high school, college and graduate students with the resources to help them make educational and career decisions.

www.sat.org Information on the SAT test. Tips for taking the SAT.

National Letter of Intent
www.national-letter.org

2006-2007
Administered by the Collegiate Commissioners Association (CCA)

**Do not sign prior to 7:00 a.m. (local time) on the following dates or
after the final signing date listed for each sport.**

SPORT		INITIAL SIGNING DATE	FINAL SIGNING DATE
____	Basketball (Early Period)	November 9, 2005	November 16, 2005
____	Basketball (Late Period)	April 12, 2006	May 17, 2006
____	Football (Midyear JC Transfer)	December 21, 2005	January 15, 2006
____	Football (Regular Period)	February 1, 2006	April 1, 2006
____	Field Hockey, Soccer, Men's Water Polo	February 1, 2006	August 1, 2006
____	All Other Sports (Early Period)	November 9, 2005	November 16, 2005
____	All Other Sports (Late Period)	April 12, 2006	August 1, 2006

(Place an "X" on the proper line.)

IMPORTANT - READ CAREFULLY

It is important to read this entire document before signing it in duplicate. One copy is to be retained by you and the other copy is to be returned to the institution, which will file a copy with the appropriate conference office. **Copies transmitted by facsimile or electronically are considered to be valid.**

---

1. **Initial Enrollment in Four-Year Institution.** This NLI is applicable only to prospective student-athletes who will be entering four-year institutions for the first time as full-time students. It is also permissible for 4-2-4 transfers who are graduating from a junior college as outlined in provision 8b to sign the NLI. With the exception of midyear transfer students in football (who must graduate at midyear for this NLI to be valid), no prospective student-athlete enrolling at midyear shall sign a NLI.

2. **Financial Aid Requirement.** At the time I sign this NLI, I must receive a written offer of athletics financial aid applicable for the entire 2006-2007 academic year from the institution named in this document. The offer shall list the terms and conditions of the award, including the amount and duration of the financial aid. (A midyear football junior college transfer must receive a written offer of athletics financial aid applicable for the remainder of the 2005-2006 academic year.) In order for this NLI to be valid, my parent/legal guardian and I must sign the NLI and the offer of athletics aid prior to submission to the institution named in this document, and any other stated conditions must also be met. If the conditions stated on the financial aid offer are not met, this NLI shall be declared null and void. An institution submitting an improper offer of athletics aid may be in violation of the NLI program and subject to sanctions.

   a. **Professional Sports Contract.** If I sign a professional sports contract in the sport in which I signed the NLI, I remain bound by the provisions of the NLI in all other sports, even if NCAA rules prohibit the institution named in this document from providing me with athletics financial aid.

3. **Provisions of Letter Satisfied.**

   a. **One-year Attendance Requirement Met.** The terms of this NLI shall be satisfied if I attend the institution named in this document for at least one academic year as a full-time student.

   b. **Junior College Graduation.** The terms of this NLI shall be satisfied if I graduate from junior college after signing this NLI either while in high school or during my first year of full-time enrollment in junior college, provided it is not the year I am scheduled to graduate from junior college.

4. **Basic Penalty.** I understand that if I do not attend the institution named in this document for one full academic year, and I enroll in another institution participating in the NLI program, I may not represent the latter institution in intercollegiate athletics competition until I have completed one full academic year in residence at the latter institution. Further, I understand I shall be charged with the loss of one season of intercollegiate athletics eligibility in all sports, except as otherwise provided in this NLI. This is in addition to any eligibility expended at any institution.

    a. **Early Signing Period Penalties.** Prospective student-athletes who will participate in football are prohibited from signing an NLI during the early signing period. A student who signs an NLI during the early period in a sport other than football will be ineligible for practice and competition in the sport of football during the student's first year of enrollment at an NLI member institution, and shall forfeit one season of eligibility in the sport of football. In circustances where a student's primary sport is not football, but the student anticipates participating in football, the student should delay signing an NLI until either the football signing period or during the late signing period for all other sports.

5. **Release Request Form.** An NLI Release Request Form may be obtained and completed in the event I wish to be released from my NLI obligation. I must sign the form, along with my parent/legal guardian, and the Director of Athletics of the institution named in this document. A Release Request Form may be obtained from the NLI website at www.national-letter.org/documents/.

    a. **Authority to Release.** A coach is not authorized to void, cancel or provide any form of release to this NLI.

    b. **Extent of the Release Request Form.** The provisions of the Release Request Form shall apply to all NLI participating institutions and shall not be conditional or selective by institution.

6. **Appeal Process.** I understand the NLI Steering Committee has been authorized to issue interpretations, settle disputes and consider petitions for a complete release from the provisions of this NLI when extenuating circumstances are determined to exist and the signing institution denies my request for complete release. I further understand the Steering Committee's decision may be appealed to the NLI Appeals Committee, whose decision shall be final and binding.

7. **Letter Becomes Null and Void.** This NLI shall be declared null and void if any of the following occur:

    a. **Admissions Requirement.** This NLI shall be declared null and void if the institution named in this document notifies me in writing that I have been denied admission or, by the opening day of classes in the fall 2006 has failed to provide me with written notice of admission, provided I have submitted a complete admission application.

        (1) It is presumed that I am eligible for admission and financial aid until information is submitted to the contrary. Thus, it is mandatory for me, upon request, to provide a transcript of my previous academic record and an application for admission to the institution named in this document.

        (2) If I am eligible for admission, but the institution named in this document defers admission to a subsequent term, the NLI shall be rendered null and void. However, if I defer my admission, this NLI remains binding.

    b. **Eligibility Requirements.** This NLI shall be declared null and void if, by the opening day of classes in the fall of 2006, I have not met (a) the institution's requirements for admissions, (b) its academic requirements for financial aid to athletes, or (c) the NCAA requirements for freshman financial aid (NCAA Bylaw 14.3) or the junior college transfer requirements.

        (1) If I become a nonqualifier (per NCAA Bylaw 14.3), this NLI shall be rendered null and void.

        (2) If I am a midyear junior college football transfer, the NLI becomes null and void if I fail to graduate from junior college at midyear. The NLI remains binding for the following fall term if I graduated, was eligible for admission and financial aid and met the junior college transfer requirements for competition for the winter or spring term, but chose to delay my admission.

    c. **One-Year Absence.** This NLI shall be null and void if I have not attended any institution (or attended an institution, including a junior college, not participating in the NLI program) for at least one academic year, provided my request for athletics financial aid for a subsequent fall term is denied. I may still apply this provision if I initially enrolled in an NLI member institution but have been absent for a period of one academic year. To apply this provision, I must file with the appropriate conference office a statement from the director of athletics at the institution named in this document that such financial aid will not be available to me for the requested fall term.

    d. **Service in the U.S. Armed Forces. Church Mission.** This NLI shall be null and void if I serve on active duty with the armed forces of the United States or on an official church mission for at least eighteen (18) months.

    e. **Discontinued Sport.** This NLI shall be null and void if the institution named in the document discontinues my sport.

f. **Recruiting Rules Violation.** If the institution (or a representative of its athletics interests) named in this document violated NCAA or conference rules while recruiting me, as found through the NCAA or conference enforcement process or acknowledged by the institution, this NLI shall be declared null and void. Such declaration shall not take place until all appeals to the NCAA or conference for restoration of eligibility have been concluded.

8. **Only One Valid NLI Permitted.** I understand that I may sign only one valid NLI, except as listed below.

    a. **Subsequent Signing Year.** If this NLI is rendered null and void under Provision 7, I remain free to enroll in any institution of my choice where I am admissible and shall be permitted to sign another NLI in a subsequent signing year.

    b. **Junior College Exception.** If I signed a NLI while in high school or during my first year of full-time enrollment in junior college, I may sign another NLI in the signing year in which I am scheduled to graduate from junior college. If I graduate, the second NLI shall be binding on me; otherwise, the original NLI, if not already satisfied, shall remain valid.

9. **Recruiting Ban After Signing.** I understand all participating conferences and institutions are obligated to respect my signing and shall cease to recruit me upon my signing this NLI. I shall notify any recruiter who contacts me that I have signed an NLI. Once I enroll in the institution with which I signed, the NLI Recruiting Ban is no longer in effect, and I shall be governed by applicable NCAA recruiting bylaws.

10. **Institutional Signatures Required Prior to Submission.** This NLI must be signed and dated by the Director of Athletics (or his/her authorized representative) before submission in duplicate to me and my parent/legal guardian for our signatures. This NLI may be mailed prior to the initial signing date. When an NLI is issued prior to the initial signing date, the "date issued" shall be the initial NLI signing date and not the date the NLI was signed or mailed by the institution.

11. **Parent/Legal Guardian Signature Required.** My parent or legal guardian is required to sign this NLI if I am less than 21 years of age at the time of my signing, regardless of my marital status. If I do not have a living parent or a legal guardian, the person who is acting in the capacity of a guardian may seek permission from the NLI Steering Committee to sign this NLI.

12. **Falsification of NLI.** If I falsify any part of this NLI or if I have knowledge that my parent or guardian falsified any part of this NLI, I understand I shall forfeit the first year of my athletics eligibility at any NLI participating institution as outlined in Provision 4.

13. **14-Day Signing Deadline.** If my parent/legal guardian and I fail to sign this NLI within 14 days from the date issued, it will be invalid. In that event, another NLI may be issued within the appropriate signing period. (NOTE: This does not apply to the early signing period from November 9-16, 2005.)

14. **Institutional Filing Deadline.** This NLI must be filed with the appropriate conference by the institution named in this document within 21 days after the date of final signature or it will be invalid. In that event, another NLI may be issued within the appropriate signing period. (NOTE: This does not apply to the early signing period from November 9-16, 2005.)

15. **No Additions or Deletions Allowed to NLI.** No additions or deletions may be made to this NLI or the Release Request Form.

16. **Official Time for Validity.** This NLI shall be considered officially signed on the final date of signature by myself or my parent/legal guardian. If no time of day is listed, the time of 11:59 p.m. will be presumed.

17. **Statute of Limitations.** This NLI is in full force and effect for a period of four (4) years, commencing with the date I sign this NLI.

18. **Nullification of Other Agreements.** My signature on this NLI nullifies any agreements, oral or otherwise, which would release me from the conditions stated within this NLI.

19. **If Coach Leaves.** I understand I have signed this NLI with the institution and not for a particular sport or individual. If the coach leaves the institution or the sports program, I remain bound by the provisions of this NLI. I understand it is not uncommon for a coach to leave his or her coaching position.

20. **Coaching Contact Prohibited at Time of Signing.** A coach or an institutional representative may not hand deliver this NLI off campus or be present off campus at the time I sign it. This NLI may be delivered by express mail, courier service, regular mail, e-mail or facsimile machine. A NLI transmitted to an institution by facsimile machine or electronically shall be considered valid.

2006-2007 NATIONAL LETTER OF INTENT (NLI)

www.national-letter.org

Name of Prospect _____

               Last   First   Middle

               (Type Proper Name, Including Middle Name or Initial)

Permanent Address _____

             Street   City   State   Zip Code

Prospect's Date of Birth _____

Submission of this NLI has been authorized by:

SIGNED   _____   _____

          Director of Athletics (or designee)   Date Issued to Prospect

         _____   _____

         Sport (Men's)   Sport (Women's)

        ☐ Check here if signee is a junior college transfer student.

This is to certify my decision to enroll at _____

                                                  Name of Institution

I certify that I have read all terms and conditions included in the four pages of this document. I have discussed them with the coach and/or other staff representatives of the institution named above, and I fully understand, accept and agree to be bound by them. (Both copies of this NLI must be signed individually.)

SIGNED (PROSPECT) _____   _____   _____

                  Prospect's Signature   Date (Mth/Day/Yr)   Time (A.M. / P.M.)

SIGNED (GUARDIAN) _____   _____   _____

          ☐ Parent or ☐ Legal Guardian Signature   Date (Mth/Day/Yr)   Time (A.M. / P.M.)

          (check one - required if student-athlete has not reached 21st birthday)

         _____   _____

         Print Name of Parent/Legal Guardian   Telephone Number (including area code)

> Falsification of a signature or a signature by a party other than the prospect and the prospect's parent/legal guardian may result in a prospect forfeiting the first year of athletics eligibility at any NLI participating institution.

Glossary

ACT (American College Test) – A standardized test measuring knowledge, comprehension and skills important for college-level work. Since it is administered to high school or community college students who wish to be admitted to a four-year college or university, the ACT can be substituted for the SAT and should be taken in the junior year of high school. It can be repeated. See your high school counselor regarding which test, the ACT or the SAT, may be right for you.

amateur – In the context of sports, a person who has not accepted payment for, or the promise of payment in any form for participation in athletics. Many rules have been established regarding the "professionalism" of prospective student-athletes. If you are in doubt about whether you qualify as an amateur, consult the athletic department for the institution you are considering and/or the association to which your school belongs, such as the NCAA, NAIA, NJCAA.

athletic association – An organization made up of colleges and/or universities formed to organize and administer all areas of intercollegiate athletics. Examples of athletic associations are the NCAA, NAIA and NJCAA.

athletic conference – A group of collegiate institutions formed for the purpose of enhancing athletic competition among member schools. Rules regarding recruiting vary among different athletic conferences and may involve different regulations regarding recruiting, competition, scholarships, etc. Find out in which athletic conferences the schools you are interested in compete. Call the specific athletic conference with any questions. Examples of athletic conferences are the Big 10, the ACC and the Pac-10.

blue-chip athlete – A superstar athlete. Blue-chip athletes are few and far between. They are typically national record holders or state champions and hold national scoring titles. Blue chippers stand above the crowd and are generally widely recruited out of high school.

class standing or rank – An indication of a high school student's academic standing relative to other students in the same grade at his or her school, generally measured by a student's grade point average (see "GPA"). For example: a student's GPA may place him/her #20 out of 300 total students in his or her class, producing a ranking in the top 10 percent (20/300 = 6.7 %).

club team – An athletic team or organization that is not formally affiliated with a school. An example of a club team for the sport of baseball is the National Little League Association and for basketball the Amateur Athletic Union (AAU). For most sports, participation on a club team can be helpful for increasing a student-athlete's exposure to college coaches and increasing his or her chances of winning a sports scholarship.

community college – Called junior colleges in some areas, community colleges are two-year institutions that may or may not offer athletic scholarships. Community colleges are an excellent alternative for high school students who are not ready to jump straight into a four-year college or university. If you are considering a particular community college, consult with its athletic department, a community college resource guide or the National Junior College Athletic Association (see NJCAA) to discover whether the college offers athletic scholarships in your sport.

contact – Any face-to-face meeting between you, the student-athlete (or your parents) and a college coach or representative with any more than "hello" passing between you. Recruiting rules regulate and limit the number and type of contacts college coaches can have with a high school student-athlete.

core course – As defined by the *NCAA Guide for the College-bound Athlete,* a core course is "...a recognized academic course (as opposed to a vocational or personal-services course) that offers fundamental instructional components in a specified area of study. Courses taught at a level below the high school's regular academic instruction level (remedial, special education or compensatory) cannot be considered core courses regardless of course content." Core-course requirements may differ from one division to another and may change depending upon the year a student-athlete first enters a collegiate institution. Consult an academic counselor early in high school to make sure you are on track to fulfill any necessary core requirements, or contact the NCAA for their guidelines.

credit – (see unit)

division – A distinction within an athletic association, for example NCAA Division I or NAIA Division II, that provides a framework concerning rules for recruiting, the number of scholarships allowed, the number of contests played, etc. under which member institutions compete. A division includes numerous athletic conferences and generally is a national organization. Different divisions have different rules. For example, NCAA Division I and II sports are able to offer athletic scholarships, while NCAA Division III schools are not. Instead, all financial aid at Division III institutions is based on need. Make sure to find out in which divisions the schools that interest you compete.

educational loans – Funds that can be borrowed by an eligible student to be used for paying education-related expenses such as tuition, books, etc. Educational loans must eventually be paid back with interest. However, interest on educational loans is usually very low and the loan recipient is not obligated to begin repayment until a specified time after leaving college. Repayment is normally structured in low monthly installments.

eligibility – The number of years a student-athlete is allowed to participate in collegiate athletics—five years total, four in any one sport. An entering freshman typically has four years of eligibility barring any unusual circumstances. After his or her participation for one year, eligibility is reduced to three years and so on until eligibility runs out.

emerging sports – To reach more equal representation for women in intercollegiate sports (see gender equity below) the NCAA recommended that eight sports be designated as emerging sports for women—archery, badminton, bowling, equestrian, rugby, squash, synchronized swimming, team handball. This designation allows these sports special status when competing in NCAA tournament play. Many of these sports are under-represented and offer an excellent opportunity for women athletes to compete in and win sports scholarships.

evaluation – An assessment made by a college coach or college representative who comes to an athletic competition or practice in which the student-athlete is participating for the purpose of evaluating his or her abilities.

FAFSA (Free Application for Federal Student Aid) – the required application for all federal aid and most need-based state and institutional aid.

financial aid – Any form of financial assistance awarded to qualified students for the purpose of paying for all or part of their college expenses.

financial aid package – The sum of any combination of financial aid in the form of grants, scholarships, educational loans and work study.

full ride – A scholarship that covers all of a student's college expenses including tuition, books, room and board; the maximum amount of scholarship money that can be awarded to an individual.

game plan – 1) Overall strategic plan that a coach develops to further the team's success. 2) Marketing strategy put together by the student-athlete to help gain the attention of college coaches and win a sports scholarship and a place on the team.

gender equity – A state of equality whereby an equivalent number of opportunities, including athletic scholarships, is available to both women and men. The national movement towards gender equity in collegiate sports programs has created more prospects for women seeking sports scholarships by increasing the number of athletic scholarships available.

grade point average (GPA) – The average grade of all classes for a student as measured by a common scale. Typically, GPA is measured using a four-point scale with A = 4.0, B = 3.0, C = 2.0, D = 1.0 and F = 0.

graduation rate – The number of students who graduate within a certain time period out of the total number of students who are in their class. For example, a school at which 950 students out of a total of 1,000 are graduating in four years of college has a graduation rate of 95 percent. Make sure you find out the graduation rate for student-athletes at the schools you are considering.

grant – A financial aid award based on the student's assessed financial need. Like a scholarship, it does not have to be repaid. Talk to financial aid counselors at the schools you are considering about grants and other financial aid application procedures.

initial contact letter – The first letter a student-athlete sends to a college coach to indicate interest in the college and its athletic program and to request more information.

Initial Eligibility Clearinghouse (IEC) – An NCAA service for evaluating a high school student-athlete's standardized test scores (SAT/ACT) and GPA to determine eligibility to compete in collegiate athletics at an NCAA institution in the freshman year. If a student-athlete wants to participate in collegiate athletics in NCAA Division I or II, he/she must be certified by the NCAA Initial Eligibility Clearinghouse. Talk to your high school counselor or coach, go to the NCAA website or call the IEC with any questions.

institution – A college or university.

junior college – (see community college)

letter of recommendation – (sometimes called recommendation) – A written testimonial by an individual describing a student's qualities, traits, skills and accomplishments for the purpose of enhancing the student's chances of being accepted into a college or athletic program and receiving a scholarship. Recommendations from a person of authority who is able to evaluate your academic and athletic skills and comment on your overall potential for success are a must for winning a sports scholarship.

major sport – A sport (also known as a revenue sport) that receives more attention relative to other sports offered at an institution. Generally, football and basketball are referred to as major sports because they tend to generate the most interest in terms of the number of fans attending their games and, therefore, the most revenue. However, many sports considered major sports at most colleges are sometimes considered minor at others.

minor sport – A sport (also known as a non-revenue sport) that usually is less well attended than major sports and does not generate as much financial support. Minor sports at one institution may be considered major sports at another.

National Association of Intercollegiate Athletics (NAIA) – An athletic association with members of approximately 300 institutions in both the U.S. and Canada. Some institutions are members in other athletic associations, as well.

National Christian College Athletic Association (NCCAA) – A collegiate athletic association that represents approximately 100 Christian colleges.

National Collegiate Athletic Association (NCAA) – The largest intercollegiate athletic association, comprised of member colleges that make rules governing eligibility, recruitment and financial aid. The NCAA has three divisions—I, II and III— in which its members compete (see divisions).

National Junior College Athletic Association (NJCAA) – An athletic association whose membership is limited to two-year community and junior colleges (see community college above). The NJCAA has three divisions in which its member institutions can compete: I, II and III. Not all community colleges belong to the NJCAA. Check the two-year institution you are considering to find out about their athletic association affiliation.

National Letter of Intent – An agreement between a college or university and a student-athlete that obligates the student to attend and/or accept an athletic scholarship to that particular institution. The National Letter of Intent program is utilized by many NCAA schools and is administered by the Collegiate Commissioners Association. There are some restrictions relating to the signing of this document that may affect your eligibility. For more information, contact the college you are considering directly or the conference to which the college belongs. Please note that not all conferences subscribe to the National Letter of Intent program.

NCAA Initial Eligibility Clearinghouse - (see Initial Eligibility Clearinghouse)

negotiate – The art of talking over an issue or problem and arriving at consensus. Successful negotiation results in a conclusion in which all the participants feel satisfied that at least part of what they asked for was granted.

nonqualifier – a student-athlete who does not meet the NCAA academic requirements to become a fully qualified Div. I or II participant. Among other restrictions, nonqualifiers cannot practice or compete with the team and cannot receive an athletic scholarship during the first year.

offer - (see scholarship offer)

official campus visit – (see recruiting trip)

off-season – The time period when your sport is not competing in its official season. Generally, in college this period is devoted to practice, practice, practice!

out-of-state tuition waiver – A collegiate institution may allow a student-athlete an out-of-state tuition waiver, thereby reducing the cost for tuition. Since most out-of-state students pay higher tuition fees, at least at public institutions, than in-state residents, this waiver is a form of financial assistance that allows the recruited student-athlete from out of state to pay the same rate as state residents.

paid visit – A visit to a collegiate institution by a prospective student-athlete paid for by the institution. There are rules regarding paid visits, including what the institution can pay for, how long the visit can be and how many paid trips a prospective student-athlete is allowed to take. Consult the institutions offering the visits or the athletic association to which the schools you're considering belong.

partial qualifier – A student-athlete who has not met all the NCAA II academic requirements. See the

NCAA website for information.

player profile sheet – A questionnaire often sent to a prospective student-athlete by a college coach to obtain academic and athletic information for further evaluation. Generally, the player profile sheet is sent to an interested student-athlete after the initial contact letter (see initial contact letter) is received by the coach. Make sure to fill out the sheet completely and return it in a timely manner. Player profile sheets are also frequently on the college website under "athletics" and your sport. On some websites you can fill out the form; on others you can download it, fill it out and then send it back to the coach.

preseason – The time period prior to the start of a sport's official season. Intense practice sessions and practice games/events are usually held during this time in preparation for the regular season.

private institution – A privately owned and funded college or university that does not receive direct financial support from the state in which it's located. Also referred to as an independent college, a private institution usually costs more to attend than a public institution.

PSAT/NMSQT (Preliminary Scholastic Assessment Test/National Merit Scholarship Qualifying Test) – This is the practice test to prepare students to take the SAT Test and is used as a guideline for early application and college potential. In addition, a sufficiently high score may result in the student's recognition and possible participation in the National Merit Scholarship Program. It is recommended that students take the test in their sophomore or junior years.

public institution – A school that is at least partially supported by public funds and tax dollars. The tuition and fees for the students are, in most cases, considerably less than those at private institutions.

qualified student-athlete – A student-athlete who is a high school graduate and has successfully met the requirements for eligibility, as mandated by the NCAA, is known as a qualified student-athlete or qualifier. Certification of a student-athlete's eligibility is determined by the NCAA Initial Eligibility Clearinghouse.

recommendation – A testimonial by an individual describing a student-athlete's qualities, traits, skills and accomplishments for the purpose of enhancing his or her chances of being accepted into a college or athletic program and receiving a scholarship.

recruit – A student-athlete solicited by a representative of a college or university for the purpose of securing his or her enrollment and participation in intercollegiate athletics at that college or university; also known as a recruited student-athlete.

recruiting service – An organization that provides exposure for student-athletes interested in playing collegiate athletics to a wide range of college coaches. Generally, these organizations charge the student-athlete a fee for their services.

recruiting trip – A visit to a college at the request of a college coach. A recruiting trip can be paid for either by the athletic program (see paid visit) or by the prospective student-athlete. There are rules regarding recruiting trips. Consult the athletic associations in which the schools compete or the athletic departments directly with any questions.

red shirt – a term given to an athlete granted an additional year of eligibility. Generally, a red-shirt year is a year in which a student-athlete is injured and not able to play the entire year, or a year in which he/she is intentionally held out from competition but is allowed to practice. Discuss the policies surrounding red shirting with the college coaches at those institutions in which you are interested.

resume – (also called the Sports Resume)—A summary of key academic and athletic information about a student-athlete, prepared for the purpose of catching a coach's attention and generating his or her interest in the student-athlete as a potential addition to the athletic program. A well-prepared resume is necessary in the prospective student-athlete's quest for scholarship dollars and is the main component of the Sports Resume Kit.

revenue sport – A collegiate sport that makes money for the athletic program and university. Revenue sports differ for each university but tend to be football and basketball at most schools. Revenue sports usually help pay for non-revenue sports that have fewer paying fans attend their contests.

road trip – The act of traveling to an away destination to compete in an athletic contest.

SAT (Scholastic Aptitude Test) – A standardized test given at prescheduled times to high school or community college students who wish to be admitted to a four-year college or university.

scholarship – Monetary award based on academic or other achievements and talents. Sometimes referred to as grants-in-aid, scholarships do not have to be repaid. Athletic scholarships are not based on need, but instead, on talent and promise. A full scholarship covers all expenses incurred in a college program, including (but not to exceed) tuition, fees, room, board and required books and supplies. A partial scholarship covers only a part of these expenses and is sometimes combined with other forms of financial aid for students who qualify.

scholarship offer – A statement to a student-athlete from a college coach notifying him or her of an institution's intent to award him or her a scholarship. A verbal commitment should always be followed by a written offer.

Sports Resume Kit – An informational packet that a student-athlete compiles about himself or herself and sends to coaches in whose colleges he or she is interested. This is the student-athlete's sales kit for showcasing his or her talents and accomplishments so that coaches know about and begin recruiting him or her.

statistics – Records or facts that are collected and classified. Athletic statistics differ from sport to sport. Some examples are goals scored, yards rushed, event times, batting average, etc. A high school or club coach can explain the statistics important in the student-athlete's sport and help compile them. The comparison of statistics between the athlete and other athletes in his or her sport helps the college coaches assess collegiate athletic potential.

student-athlete – A person enrolled in an academic institution for the purpose of gaining an education who, at the same time, also participates in athletics.

superstar – A person with extraordinary athletic talent, along with high-profile scores, times and ratings. High school superstars are usually ranked state-wide or nationally in their sport. Highly recruited by mostly Division I colleges and universities, superstars also are referred to as blue-chip athletes.

Title IX – Part of the Education Amendments passed by Congress in 1972 that called for equal opportunity for female student-athletes. Today, due to new, stricter rules and the enforcement of Title IX, colleges and universities have generally moved towards gender equity, creating a wealth of sports opportunities for female athletes (see gender equity).

transcript – A document that lists a student's grades for each class of instruction for each grade level. Generally, high school transcripts must be sent along with an application for admission to college. It is also a good idea to send a copy of your transcript with your Sports Resume Kit to each college coach in whose program you are interested. If you have attended more than one high school, you will need to make sure you have transcripts from each.

tuition – The amount charged to a college student for enrollment. This amount is generally different for each school and sometimes depends upon whether the student enrolled resides in-state or out-of-state. Tuition generally does not include expenses such as books or room and board.

tuition fee-waiver – (see out-of-state tuition waiver)

undergraduate – A college student who is in the process of completing the course work necessary for obtaining a bachelor's degree. Upon graduating from college, an undergraduate becomes a graduate.

unofficial campus visit – student-athletes are allowed unlimited visits to colleges as long as expenses are paid by the student-athlete, not by the institution. Unofficial campus visits can be taken before the senior year.

unit – Also called a credit, a standard of measure utilized by academic institutions in an effort to quantify the amount of course work a student has completed.

varsity – The most important or highest level of sport at a high school, college or university. Junior varsity teams are usually made up of younger, less experienced players who are building skills and maturing so they can enter varsity competition.

walk-on – 1) To try out for a collegiate athletic team after you have been admitted to a college that didn't recruit you. 2) A student-athlete trying out for a college team whose coach did not recruit him or her prior to admission to the school. There have been numerous success stories of students who were not recruited by a particular program out of high school but who enrolled at the school, tried out and made the team, and eventually received an athletic scholarship. If you are not offered a scholarship to the school you want to attend, ask the college coach about walking-on, with the possibility of earning a scholarship at a later date. Sometimes an interested coach may want to see a student-athlete perform with the team before making a commitment and will invite him or her to walk on after being admitted.

work-study – A part-time job, most often on campus, during the school year that enables the student-athlete to earn money. Usually work-study is part of a financial aid package. Although tough to handle while also playing a varsity collegiate sport, work-study can be done. Talk to the financial aid office and college coach about the possibilities.

Index